The Academic Library and the Net Gen Student

Making the Connections

SUSAN GIBBONS

AMERICAN LIBRARY ASSOCIATION

Chicago   2007

Design and composition by ALA Editions in Trebuchet and Palatino typefaces using InDesign CS2 for a PC platform.

Printed on 50-pound white offset, a pH-neutral stock, and bound in 10-point cover stock by McNaughton & Gunn.

The paper used in this publication meets the minimum requirements of American National Standard for Information Sciences—Permanence of Paper for Printed Library Materials, ANSI Z39.48-1992. ∞

Library of Congress Cataloging-in-Publication Data

Gibbons, Susan (Susan L.), 1970–
    The academic library and the net gen student : making the connections / Susan Gibbons.
        p.   cm.
    Includes bibliographical references and index.
    ISBN 978-0-8389-0946-1 (alk. paper)
    1. Academic libraries—Information technology. 2. Academic libraries—Aims and objectives. 3. Education, Higher—Effect of technological innovations on. 4. Technology and youth. I. Title.
    Z675.U5G49 2007
    027.7—dc22   2007013302

ISBN-13: 978-0-8389-0946-1
ISBN-10: 0-8389-0946-9

Printed in the United States of America

11   10   09   08   07   5   4   3   2   1

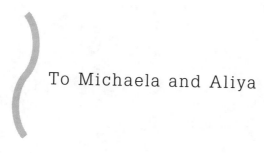

To Michaela and Aliya

CONTENTS

PREFACE

THE PATH THAT LED ME TO WRITE THIS BOOK HAS been anything but straight and clear. It began in 2003 when I was the director of digital initiatives for the River Campus Libraries of the University of Rochester. David Lindahl, a former Xerox PARC researcher, and I headed up the newly formed Digital Initiatives Unit, and we were each dealing with quite different problems. David wanted to bring a technique he had used at Xerox PARC, work-practice study, to the libraries. A work-practice study is a method of fine-grained observation and documentation of people at work based on traditional anthropological participant observation; two examples of work-practice study are Wenger (1998) and Goodwin (1994). Through the work-practice study methodology, David believed, we could better align the libraries' digital tools and web presence with the real, rather than perceived, needs of our users. Unfortunately, a work-practice study requires the expertise of a research social scientist, such as an anthropologist; although a superb idea, it was going to be difficult to convince the libraries to spend their limited budget hiring such a person.

My charge was to establish an institutional repository (IR) for the university. An IR was both a technology and a service that really pushed libraries into a new territory and presupposed a relationship between academic libraries and faculty that was heretofore quite rare. Although the concept of an IR made sense on paper, did the faculty really want one?

David and I came upon a single solution for our two very different problems, which was to write a grant that would provide the funding to hire a social scientist for a year, during which time we could conduct a faculty work-practice study in order to better understand how an IR might fit into the existing work practices of faculty. The Institute of Museum and Library Services graciously funded our project as a 2003 National Leadership Grant. When we advertised for a research social scientist, we were incredibly fortunate to find Nancy Fried Foster, who had a PhD in applied anthropology from Columbia University and a diploma in social anthropology from Oxford, had conducted research in small indigenous communities in Brazil and Papua New Guinea, and had experience studying work environments.

Dr. Foster, as well as the experience of the grant, exceeded all of our expectations. Using various ethnographic techniques, we gained incredible insight into how our faculty in different disciplines conducted their research. From this information we were able to see the many ways we could improve our IR to better align it with the needs of our faculty (Foster and Gibbons 2005).

The great success of the faculty work-practice study whetted our appetite for more. The River Campus Libraries' administration, of which I was now the assistant dean for public services and collection development, asked Foster to extend her time with us. Her new task was to help us better understand our undergraduate students. The undergraduate research project, which ran from 2004 to 2006, focused on how undergraduate students did their academic work. To address this topic, the project, which involved more than thirty members of the libraries' staff, used a mixture of methodologies—including photo elicitation, mapping diaries, and retrospective interviews—to develop a holistic picture of the lives of our students. From this larger picture, we then tried to understand how the libraries' services, facilities, resources, and digital presence fit or could fit into the students' academic and social lives.

As the project progressed, I could not help but notice that the students were awash in different technologies, ranging from iPods to cell phones to Xboxes. At first I dismissed these technologies as incidental or little more than distractions from the core of the students' academic work. However, as the information from the project began mounting, so too did the evidence that my personal biases were preventing me from really understanding technology's critical and myriad roles in the social and academic lives of today's undergraduate students. Consequently, I made a conscious effort to put my preconceptions aside and stop assuming that my college years were anything like those of today's students. I began to watch carefully and listen more attentively to the students, and I started to read whatever I could find that would shed light on how college-age Americans use technology.

It did not take long before I realized that my preconceptions were completely wrong. Cell phones, iPods, wikis, instant messenger, and online games are not ancillary to traditional academic tools such as books, laptops, and lecture halls. Rather, these technologies have become essential to the students' academic tool kit. Moreover, if we wanted our academic libraries to continue to be a vital part of the academic success of undergraduate students, we had to embrace these technologies as well.

This book is a manifestation of what I learned on this journey and my thoughts about the ways academic libraries can better align themselves with the actual, rather than perceived, needs of today's students with respect to technology.

ACKNOWLEDGMENTS

I THANK ALL OF MY COLLEAGUES AT THE UNIVER-
sity of Rochester Libraries, who are constant sources of in-
spiration, particularly Dean Ronald Dow, who has been
unwavering in his support and encouragement. I am very appreciative of the
editorial support from ALA Editions and John Thomas.

This book would never have come to fruition were it not for my husband,
Michael. He has been my sounding board, personal editor, and greatest fan
throughout the entire process. Thank you!

INTRODUCTION

AFTER CENTURIES OF RELATIVE STABILITY, MORE than a few people within the higher education community are questioning the usefulness, viability, and longevity of academic libraries in an increasingly digital world. With the emergence of digitization technologies, computers, and word processors in the 1970s came aspirations for a "paperless" society in which the entire corpus of the world's literature would be at one's fingertips (*Business Week* 1975). Campus planners saw a not-too-distant future where the "need for ever increasing central campus space for the library system would not be necessary" (Matier and Sidle 1992, 21). Although the initial expectations of a digital-only academic library quieted down toward the turn of the century, the predictions received new life with the 2004 announcement of the Google Print project.[1] Google's ambitious plan to digitize all the books in the library collections of Harvard University, Stanford University, the University of Michigan, Oxford University, and the New York Public Library caused many to question once again the academic library's raison d'être.

It is not too difficult to understand why the elimination of a college's library collection might seem plausible, if not inevitable. Information is indeed rapidly moving online. One discipline after another has voiced its preference for online access to the journal literature, which began in the sciences, moved into the social sciences, and is presently creeping into the humanities. And now Google Print, renamed Google Book Search, promises to do the same for the monographic literature, following on the heels of some smaller-scale electronic book collections such as NetLibrary (www.netlibrary.com) and ebrary (www.ebrary.com). Even if the bulk of the world's literature takes decades in transition from the print to digital medium, the end of the primacy of libraries as the warehouses of the world's literature is well within sight.

Meanwhile, academic libraries across the country are building collections that are increasingly more similar than dissimilar. With an escalating number of published journals and monographs and a diminishing cadre of collection development staff, the days of an exclusively title-by-title selection of a library collection have become nearly impossible. On the book side of acquisitions, more and more reliance is placed on approval plans to ensure that the "key works" of a discipline are automatically purchased. The cost and complexity of the dual electronic and paper journal world create an increasing number of bundled purchases, such as the Elsevier "Big Deal" and packages available from IEEE, Wiley, and Springer. Although the approval plans and journal bundles bring some much-needed efficiency to the acquisitions and collection development tasks, they also increase the level of uniformity of collections across academic libraries. Thus, the college down the road seems to have access to the same core set of journals, article databases, and books as yours. So, in this digital age, where physical distance and boundaries are apparently irrelevant, why shouldn't administrators at the two colleges consider consolidating their two libraries into one?

It is no surprise that a balanced budget is the issue that most worries college presidents (Selingo 2005, A26). Financial downturns at both the state and federal levels have caused some to wonder exactly what it means to be a public higher education institution. The state of Michigan, for example, provides only 18% of the University of Michigan–Ann Arbor's revenues, and the University of Virginia receives a mere 8% of its budget from the state coffers (Dillon 2005, 12). Private higher education institutions are not immune from these financial concerns. Modest to poor returns on the investment of endowments have constricted the rapid growth funded by the robust economy of the mid-1990s. Even those institutions with generous endowments can find themselves constrained by narrowly written endowment agreements, which, for example, provide ample funding for new buildings but not a cent for their maintenance.

The shrinking funding sources for higher education have not been offset by equally diminishing costs. Students are an ever more demanding consumer, expecting robust technological infrastructures, state-of-the-art facilities, and ample opportunities and resources to explore their many-faceted interests. Near the center of this fiscal tug of war sits the university's library, often sitting on prime campus real estate and requiring a budget that annually exceeds the rate of inflation just to sustain its baseline (Van Orsdel and Born 2005). Inside the library rest hundreds of thousands, often millions, of paper books and journals. When campus administrators hear the statistic that 20% of a library collection accounts for 90% of its use (Dempsey 2006), why should they not imagine a library with a much smaller footprint, supplemented by vast digital collections? Moreover, would this smaller physical library not translate into smaller operating and personnel budgets for the library? Potential cost savings abound!

All of these forces have combined to push academic libraries into far less stable terrain than in decades, even centuries, past. The future of academic libraries and academic librarianship is unclear to some and a mystery to most. Still, this book makes the bold assumption that there is a real, vibrant future for academic libraries. But that future requires a realignment of the services, collections, and resources of academic libraries with the academic needs of their unique higher education community, in particular undergraduate students.

The premise that academic libraries will continue to have a vibrant, meaningful role in higher education into the foreseeable future is not a given. Consequently, this book begins with a brief foray into business theories to compare academic libraries with organizations that have failed in periods of transition and with those that have succeeded. From this perspective we craft a potential mission for academic libraries that is agile, meaningful, and in many ways consistent with the evolution of academic librarianship.

At the heart of this mission rests the need to align an academic library's services, facilities, and resources with the real, rather than perceived, needs of its unique higher education community. It is only natural for organizations to define themselves by their traditions, strengths, and history. However, with real competition growing in the library marketplace and higher education undergoing transformational shifts, an academic library cannot continue to view itself through the narrow lens of past practices. Such an approach will essentially guarantee the marginalization of academic libraries. Rather, the mission of an academic library should *follow* the needs of its patrons, even if it means changing some of the library's core functions and services.

Traditionally, the faculty members of a university are the high-end customers of an academic library. Although the teaching and research needs of the faculty should always remain a priority for libraries, this should not be to the exclusion of a high level of support for the learning and research needs of the undergraduate students. Due in large part to some foundational shifts in the academic and social practices of today's undergraduate students brought about by accelerating advances in technology, our affinity with the students grows weaker. A significant abyss is forming between the undergraduate students, members of the "Net Generation," and the rest of campus. To remain relevant and continue to support the teaching, learning, and research agenda of our higher education institutions, it is imperative for academic libraries to begin closing this gap, if for no other reason than that these Net Generation students are our future graduate students and faculty members.

Chapters 3–6 demonstrate some ways the mission of an academic library can proceed and develop from the needs of its most junior patrons, the Net Generation undergraduate students, by focusing narrowly on their use of digital technology. Although the Net Generation's seemingly effortless use of technology often defines them, it is important to remember that technology is just one lens of a multifaceted prism through which we can come to understand our students better. Other facets could include familial relations, popular culture, and civic service, to name just a few.

Each of these chapters follows a three-step process. The first step is an examination of a new technological genre, including online gaming, blogs, and social bookmarking. The second step pulls together information from the growing body of literature to make evidence-based observations about how students are using these new technological suites in their social and academic practices. The final step derives from this information some suggestions about how an academic library could change in order to adapt, accommodate, and remain relevant to its students as they weave technologies into their academic and social lives. The concluding chapter takes a few steps back to suggest some guiding principles that can help sustain adaptive and agile academic libraries into the foreseeable future.

NOTE

1. See *Google checks out library books:* http://www.google.com/press/pressrel/print_library .html.

CHAPTER ONE

The Mission of an Academic Library

TO BEGIN TO CRAFT A VISION FOR THE FUTURE OF academic libraries, we start with an examination of some organizational business theories. The use of business theory is not to suggest that academic libraries should be managed more like for-profit businesses. Rather, there are business theories that transcend the profit/ nonprofit designations and can be of value in understanding the changing landscape of academic libraries. Specifically, Clayton Christensen's *Innovator's Dilemma* (2000) offers great insight to how well-established, well-managed organizations can still fail, and in *Good to Great* (2001) and its sequel (2005) Jim Collins demonstrates why some organizations have achieved unparalleled success. Borrowing from these perspectives, we can compare academic libraries with organizations that have failed in periods of transition and with those that have prospered.

Academic Libraries and Disruptive Technologies

Christensen's *Innovator's Dilemma* is about the "failure of companies to stay atop their industries when they confront certain types of market and technological change" (2000, xi). His study focuses not on organizations that were weak in some fundamental area but rather on well-managed, customer-centered organizations that still collapsed or lost primacy in the marketplace, such as Sears Roebuck, Digital Equipment Corporation, Xerox, and Bethlehem Steel Corporation. In each of these cases, and many more, the organization did what the traditional management literature recommends: it stayed focused on its core competencies, responded to the demands of its high-end customers, and invested in new technologies and processes. What each firm failed to do, though, was pay early and serious attention to "disruptive technologies" within the marketplace.

Christensen distinguishes between sustaining and disruptive technologies. Sustaining technologies "improve the performance of established products, along the dimensions of performance that mainstream customers in major markets have historically valued." In other words, sustaining technologies make existing product lines better, such as the move from black-and-white to color photography. Disruptive technologies, on the other hand, bring a new proposition to the market that is usually cheaper and more convenient (2000, xviii). The movement away from film-based photography to digital photography is a good example, as are the replacement of travel agents by online travel sites and bank tellers by ATMs.

What makes a disruptive technology so disruptive is that it (1) targets customers who in the past had not been able to "do it themselves" for lack of money or skills; (2) targets customers who will welcome a simpler product; and (3) helps customers do more easily and effectively what they are already trying to do (Christensen, Aaron, and Clark 2001, 32). Often disruptive technologies enter the marketplace as inferior substitutes to established product lines. Consequently, the technologies are initially dismissed and ignored by the established firms, which continue to focus on sustaining improvements to their own existing product lines. At some point, however, the established firms overshoot their market by giving "customers more than they need or ultimately are willing to pay for" (Christensen 2000, xix). Meanwhile, the disruptive technology has slowly been improving and chipping away at the low end of the market. By the time the established firms are able to see the full potential and threat of the disruptive technology, it is too late for them to react.

Although the theory of disruptive technology may appear quite foreign to academic librarianship, it may actually go a long way to explain much of the recent upheaval caused by the Internet (Lafferty and Edwards 2004; Lewis 2004). It is not inconceivable that the Internet and the ever-expanding services built upon it are in fact disruptive technologies for academic libraries.

Historically academic libraries have never been easy places for an undergraduate student to traverse, intellectually and even physically, but the student had no alternative. Academic progress rested upon gaining some degree of familiarity with the content and services of the campus library. Today, because of the Internet and Web, this same student has some very real alternatives, as demonstrated in the areas of ready reference services and book and article discovery tools.

While libraries make incremental and sustaining improvements to their reference services, such as the incorporation of online chat software for virtual reference, competitors are harnessing the power of the Internet to create easier and more convenient ways of obtaining information. For example, Google Answers had a cadre of more than five hundred researchers available to answer reference questions when a trip to the reference desk at the library was too cumbersome (e.g., bad weather or difficult parking), when the library was closed, or when the virtual reference service was not staffed. The easiest reaction for librarians to the entry of Google Answers and other alternative reference services into the library's traditional territory is to focus on the perceived inferior quality of those services. But remember, a disruptive technology usually begins as an inferior substitute, yet one that is easier and more convenient. Moreover, a 2003 qualitative analysis of reference answers provided by Google Answers and Cornell University reference librarians found that, "although the Cornell reference librarians scored higher overall than did the freelance researchers working for Google, their scores were not significantly better" (Kenney et al. 2003). Although Google decided to shut down its Google Answers service in November 2006,[1] there are still ChaCha search (www.chacha.com), Yahoo! Answers (answers.yahoo.com), and others. So even with Google Answers' demise the lesson remains the same: the challenge to the designation of the library reference desk as information provider of choice is both real and quite competitive.

When a student is searching for relevant books on his topic of research, Amazon.com can be a good, often superior, alternative to the library's online catalog. As the student searches for books using keyword terms, Amazon .com's algorithms are constantly churning in the background and pushing tailored suggestions for other books to consider: "Customers who bought this item also bought . . ." and "See all xxx books citing this book." The student also benefits from the many reader reviews that offer valuable information for assessing quality and relevance. Although the library's online catalog can also link a user to related books using the subject headings, this relationship is usually hidden behind the poorly labeled "Subject(s)" link. (See fig. 1-1.) What about this link would make users believe that it is a pathway to books of a similar topic? Libraries could create the equivalent of Amazon.com's recommendation system by using circulation patterns at their institutions or across several institutions, which could be made anonymous. But, as Thomas and McDonald so accurately observe, "Dogmatic library protection of privacy inhibits library support for . . . online trust-based transactions that are increasingly common online" (2005, 101). Consequently, potentially rich and immensely useful data are allowed to remain fallow.

Once our student makes a list of interesting books from Amazon.com, he can check for the titles in his library's online catalog and may discover that some of the books are owned by the library. Some are, however, likely to be checked out, which is understandable since his classmates are all working on

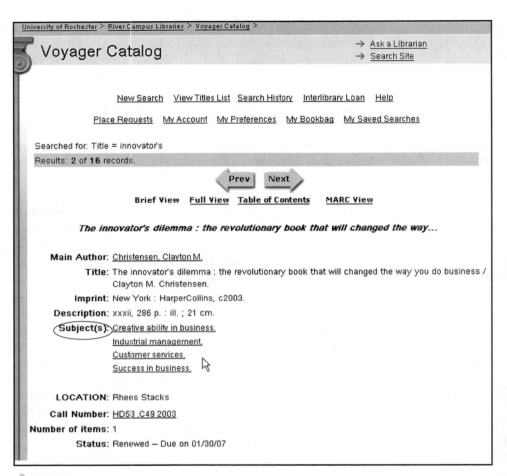

〉 **FIGURE 1-1**
Book record from the University of Rochester's Voyager Catalog

the same general research topic. Other books on his desiderata list may have a status of "missing," and still others may be available only through interlibrary loan. At this point, the student will determine what is most important to him in this situation, money or time. If money is the scarce resource in his life, he will need to initiate book recalls and interlibrary loan requests and hope that the books make it to him in time to write his paper. If instead his scarce resource is actually time (e.g., paper due in two or three days), then Amazon.com is his most efficient solution. Thanks to twenty-four-hour delivery options and Amazon.com's Search Inside functionality, he will have books that he has been able to determine are highly relevant to his research topic delivered right to his doorstep. If you doubt that this is happening, take a moment to visit your campus post office to see how many Amazon.com boxes come through each day.

More efficient discovery alternatives are not limited to the monographic side of a library's collection. A student in need of scholarly articles for her research paper need no longer plod her way through the library's long lists of article databases and electronic journals. Why should she conduct consecutive searches in one database after another when Google Scholar (scholar.google.com) permits her to search across the content of many of the library's licensed databases simultaneously? Articles published or distributed by the American Chemical Society, Elsevier, Project Muse, Springer, Blackwell, JSTOR, American Physical Society, University of Chicago Press, and many others are all searchable through the simple yet powerful interface of Google Scholar. Because Google Scholar can be configured to work with her library's "OpenURL" linking technology, she has full access to many of the same texts she would locate via the native database interfaces.

In summary, the Internet marketplace offers viable, easier, and more efficient alternatives to many of the traditional cornerstones of academic libraries. Each of these examples shows a technology that is allowing patrons to do things that in the recent past required a librarian's assistance or library resources to accomplish. If academic libraries are considered warehouses of information and academic librarians the gatekeepers of that information, then the Internet may indeed be a disruptive technology for academic libraries.

Applying the Hedgehog Concept

Disruptive technologies offer challenges, but the future of academic libraries appears brighter when studied in the light of Collins's *Good to Great*. Collins examined the eleven Fortune 500 businesses that were able to become market leaders within their business sectors and sustain their positions for fifteen years or more. From this in-depth analysis he identified some common factors for success. One of these is what he terms the "hedgehog concept." The essence of this concept is an organization's ability "to attain piercing clarity about how to produce the best long-term results, and then exercising the relentless discipline to say 'No thank you' to opportunities that fail the hedgehog test" (2005, 17). In other words, Collins found a disciplined, well-focused core at the center of each of these successful organizations.

The hedgehog concept has three overlapping circles. The intersection of these three circles is the audacious goal that should be the constant focus of an organization. (See fig. 1-2.) In the first circle is passion—"what you are deeply passionate about." Although librarians have been criticized for their rigidity, obsession for perfection, and lack of clothing panache, their passion for their work is rarely in doubt. This passion flows through our unwavering defense of uncensored access to information, intellectual freedom, and lifelong learning, among many other core principles. Librarians may lack a shared understanding of how to actualize these core values and principles, but the passion to do so is never lacking.

The second circle focuses on what an organization can be the best at in the world. Collins is careful to clarify that this is not an intention or aspiration for the organization but rather a clear understanding of what it realistically can be the best at (2001, 197–204). This may seem quite a bold charge, yet academic libraries have an easier time than most organizations in defining this vision. Each academic library has an irreplaceable contribution because its mission is

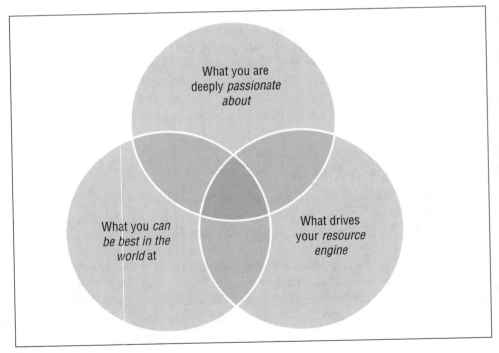

FIGURE 1-2
Diagram of the hedgehog concept. Reproduced with permission from *Good to Great and the Social Sectors,* by Jim Collins.

defined by the unique academic institution it serves. It is the distinctiveness of each higher education institution that in turn demands that each academic library be unique. Consequently, the focus of an academic library is to be the best library in the world at serving the teaching, learning, and research needs of its higher education institution. What those needs are requires further refinement at an institutional level, but it is because of this need for localization that Google and Amazon.com, though competitive, cannot do a better job than an academic library at serving the needs of a unique academic community.

The third circle is "what drives your resource engine," which Collins (2001) simplifies into a single ratio of profit per *x*, such as profit per store, profit per employee, or profit per ton of finished steel. This concept is a bit harder to apply to an academic library because libraries have neither easily measured outputs nor a profit orientation. Although academic libraries have attempted to develop metrics and comparators with other libraries, such as material expenditures and circulation statistics, these are not the most meaningful, mission-centered success measures for an academic library. An academic library should not be compared to other academic libraries; instead, it should be measured by its contribution to the learning, teaching, and research that occurs at its home institution. This local impact, obviously, can be quite difficult to measure, and consequently not enough libraries try. Collins does not, however, let libraries and the rest of the social sector off of the hook so easily. All organizations must hold themselves "accountable for progress in outputs, *even if those outputs defy measurement.*" He goes on to explain:

> It doesn't really matter whether you can quantify your results. What matters is that you rigorously assemble *evidence*—quantitative or qualitative—to track your progress. If the evidence is primarily qualitative, think like a trial lawyer assembling the combined body of evidence. If the evidence is primarily quantitative, then think of yourself as a laboratory scientist assembling and assessing the data. (2005, 5)

This presents quite a challenge for academic libraries, yet one that is not impossible when a library is passionate about being the world's best at serving the teaching, learning, and research needs of its unique home institution. Potential quantitative and qualitative outcome measures for an academic library must be tailored to the distinct mission the library serves at its higher education institution. A few examples are presented below, ranging from the more to less common, to demonstrate the breadth of possibilities. In each case, it would be important for a library to track changes in these metrics from year to year.

number of book circulations

number of website hits

number of article downloads

number of requests for personalized reference assistance

number of requests for class bibliographic instruction sessions

number of positive mentions of the library in the student newspaper

level of library's invited participation in campuswide task forces, projects, and search committees that deal directly with teaching, learning, and research

number of interlibrary loan requests for materials already owned by the library, which is an indicator of the clarity and intuitiveness of a library's material location tools

faculty opinions, regularly solicited, regarding the quality of student research and information-seeking skills

number of classes that use special collections materials

number of library acknowledgments in works published by faculty

how frequent the library is a selling point in a new faculty hire

Taken as a whole, Collins's hedgehog concept provides an academic library a framework with which to bring clarity to mission and measures for success.

Crafting a Mission

So how does one view academic libraries within the combined lens of Christensen's and Collins's works? Christensen reinforces the fear that the Internet will replace libraries as the information provider of choice for most people—something that has already happened with most undergraduate students. In 2002, 73% of U.S. college students reported using the Internet more than the library (Jones 2002, 12), and this number has surely risen. OCLC's 2005 report "Perceptions of Libraries and Information Resources" found that 58% of this country's young adults ages 18 to 24 consider themselves either "extremely familiar" or "very familiar" with online search engines. Only 44% could say the same for the physical library and, oddly, a mere 20% for the online library (De Rosa et al. 2005, 1–7).

The replacement of libraries by the Web as the information provider of choice may be impossible to prevent. Ceding the role of primary information provider does not, however, diminish the purpose of an academic library unless that library's mission is to be the information provider of choice. If academic libraries and librarianship are instead defined by a much broader mission, one that is not solely defined by access to information, then the Web will not displace libraries so easily. To explain this distinction, it is helpful to first recognize the differences between information and knowledge.

In their incredibly insightful book *The Social Life of Information* (2000), John Seely Brown and Paul Duguid articulate some important distinctions between information and knowledge. Their first point is that, although information can exist independently, knowledge requires a knower, as illustrated by the awkwardness of replacing the word "information" with "knowledge" in the phrase "I found some great information about that on the Web." Second, although information is quite easy to share, locate, and possess, knowledge is much harder to transfer. Someone can give you information but cannot so easily give you knowledge. Finally, "knowledge is something we digest rather than merely hold," and this assimilation takes time and practice. From these differences, Brown and Duguid conclude that a "shift toward knowledge may (or should) represent a shift toward people. . . . [I]ncreasingly, as the abundance of information overwhelms us all, we need not simply more information, but people to assimilate, understand, and make sense of it" (2000, 120–21).

Thus, the distinction between information and knowledge points toward a mission for academic libraries that cannot be replaced by the Web. Some information is now easier to obtain from the Web than from a library, but the creation and assimilation of knowledge still require the involvement of people, and academic librarians are perfectly positioned to provide these services.

Librarians as Translators

Academic librarians, particularly subject specialists, are important as both disciplinary insiders and outsiders. In large academic libraries, it is the norm that a subject specialist or bibliographer has both a master's in library science and an advanced degree in the subject he or she serves. This advanced training helps assimilate librarians into the norms and practices of the discipline, whether it is history, sociology, physics, or engineering. These librarians are also outsiders, however, because they do not practice the discipline on a daily basis.

The importance of this dual role of insider and outsider can be critical in the successful transmission of knowledge between professor and student. One way to view a student's undergraduate years is as a period of acculturation into the discourse of his selected discipline. Simmons describes disciplinary discourse as "the ways that members of a particular discourse community write, read, speak, and research, as well as the assumptions that they make and the epistemologies with which they craft their argument" (2005, 297). Unfortunately, faculty are sometimes unable to articulate the norms of their discipline. "As insiders in a community of practice, scholars in a discipline may find it difficult to see their disciplinary practices as anything but natural—the 'way things are'" (Simmons 2005, 304). But the librarian can act as a translator between the apprentices (students) and discipline masters (professors).

The faculty's lament that students cannot write and conduct research is heard with every incoming class of freshmen. Although some incoming students do in fact lack the ability to write and conduct research well, perhaps sometimes the problem is subtler than poor skills. In some instances, what the faculty member sees as poor writing may actually be the student's inability to write as a member of the discipline would be expected to write. Perhaps what the faculty member sees as poor research skills is actually the student's inability to conduct research in the style of the discipline.

As both insiders and outsiders, librarians reside in a unique space. Librarians can serve as guides and aids as students seek to understand the various disciplines they encounter through their coursework. When the student selects a major, the librarian can then assist in the process by which the student becomes acculturated to a discipline. "By articulating and making visible the epistemological differences in research in the disciplines, librarians can facilitate students' understanding and their scholarly work within a particular discipline" (Simmons 2005, 305). Few other groups on an academic campus can serve this same insider/outsider role.

Another way to think of librarians' role on an academic campus is as part of academic scaffolding that supports the endeavors of students. "Knowledge is information that has been internalized and integrated into our frameworks. To facilitate a student's learning we [the academy] need to design spaces that encourage and scaffold conversations that do that" (Brown 2002, 54). Student learning need not be limited to the classroom and conversations with faculty. If designed properly, the library can be an effective learning space and, more important, librarians can be a part of the scaffolding that helps turn information into knowledge. Or, as Lankes and Silverstein (2006) suggest, libraries can be a key part of the conversations that create knowledge.

From all of this it is possible to derive a mission for academic libraries that is both essential and irreplaceable by technology. The goal of an academic library is to be the best in the world at serving the unique teaching, learning, and research needs of its home academic institution by being active participants in the creation, transmission, and dissemination of knowledge.

The Internet and Web cannot replace the academic library because, although technology can be a better information provider, it cannot substitute for the essential role of humans in the creation, transmission, and dissemination of knowledge. Many faculty cannot take over the roles of academic librarians because they are too much a part of a discipline and are unable to articulate what to them is naturally the "way things are."

Success in this role as translator, however, necessitates an in-depth understanding of faculty and students. Although librarians, particularly those with faculty status, have developed a connection and relationship with teaching and research faculty, increasingly their affinity with students grows weaker. Today's undergraduate students operate academically and socially in ways that are fundamentally different from librarians, both now and when the librarians were undergraduates. Students operate so differently, in fact, that they have begun to shift the foundations that underpin higher education.

Although disruptive technologies may uncrown libraries as the best information provider, there is still a viable and crucial function for academic libraries into the foreseeable future. If an academic library is truly committed to being the best in the world at serving the teaching, learning, and research needs of its unique host institution and to being a key part of the scaffolding for the creation, transmission, and dissemination of knowledge, then it is imperative for that library to really come to know and understand its youngest patrons, the undergraduate students. We cannot simply rest on our knowledge that the students, members of the rising Net Generation, are different. We must understand how and why and embrace those differences—not ignore, reject, or dismiss them. Our role as translators requires us to meet undergraduate students where they are, mentally, physically, and virtually, and help bring them to where the faculty reside. If we cannot begin to deepen our affinity with undergraduate students now, how much more daunting and difficult the task will be when they become our Net Generation faculty.

NOTE

1. See http://googleblog.blogspot.com/2006/11/adieu-to-google-answers.html.

CHAPTER TWO

The Net
Generation

TO FULFILL THE ROLE OF TRANSLATOR BETWEEN
faculty and students, it is imperative that academic libraries come to understand their undergraduate students as
they understand their faculty, or at least to try. To develop an appreciation for
the Net Generation, today's undergraduate students, it is useful to see them as
just one of several generations that inhabits any college campus. It can be easy
to view a university community as having two distinct groupings, students
and nonstudents, but in reality a campus is the blending of several generations
that blur the bipolar student/nonstudent distinction. Although it can seem
to be a gross generalization, each generation is truly distinct because of the
shared experiences and history that binds its members.

The Net Generation has been given many labels: Generation Y, Millennials
(Howe and Strauss 2000; Strauss and Howe 2006), Echo Boomers, Generation
M (Israel 2006), and Generation Me (Twenge 2006). We are still awaiting the
maturation of the Net Generation's identity, but some promising predictions
have already been made. According to Strauss and Howe, three basic rules
apply to a rising generation in "nontraditional societies, such as America, that
allow young people some freedom to define what it means to be young." The
first is that the rising generation "breaks with the styles and attitudes of the
young-adult generation." The second is that the rising generation "corrects
for what it perceives as the excesses of the current midlife generation," who
are their parents. And finally, the rising generation "fills the social role being
vacated by the departing elder generation" (Strauss and Howe 2006, 47–48).
With this framework, we can begin to see how the Net Generation will be like
and unlike the generations that have preceded it.

Although there is no universally agreed-on classification of generations
within the United States, most breakdowns are similar to the one used by
Howe and Strauss in *Millennials Rising* (2000) and *Millennials and the Pop Culture*

(2006). The G.I. Generation encompasses those Americans born between 1901 and 1924. This generation, also labeled the "Greatest Generation" in a recent work by Tom Brokaw, is primarily defined by their perseverance through the Depression era of the 1930s and their valiant sacrifices in World War II (Strauss and Howe 2006, 18). Out of necessity, the women of the G.I. Generation entered the workforce (outside the home) in unprecedented numbers. Higher education was radically altered by this generation when the G.I. Bill provided returning soldiers affordable opportunities to acquire a college education, which brought heretofore unseen numbers of new students onto college campuses.

The Silent Generation (1925–42) was very much overshadowed by the G.I. Generation. This generation "grew up as the suffocated children of war and depression." They were too young to be war heroes and too old to fully enjoy the free spirit of the 1960s. Their early adult years were marked by conformity and risk aversion, and their golden years are ones of unprecedented personal wealth (Strauss and Howe 2006, 18).

In contrast, the Baby Boomers (1943–60) have been anything but silent. The "proud creation of postwar optimism," the Boomers represent the largest American generation to date (Strauss and Howe 2006, 19). In spite of the cold war, Boomers have remained optimistic about the future, with a strong sense of entitlement. This sense of entitlement continues to grow as the Boomers enter retirement with high expectations for Social Security and Medicare benefits. During the 1960s and the Vietnam War, the Baby Boomers unleashed a remarkable wave of rebellion, self-confidence, and experimentation.

Generation X (1961–81), on the other hand, grew up in a far less optimistic period. The free-spirited nature of the 1960s was largely dampened by the AIDS epidemic and the nation's "war on drugs" (Strauss and Howe 2006, 19). Their childhood was defined, in large part, by rising divorce rates and broken families. The poster child for the Generation X childhood is the latchkey kid— a child with a key tied around his neck, returning from school to an empty home, waiting for his parents to return from work. Generation Xers are often characterized as individualistic, self-reliant, and overly pessimistic.

Using the rules Strauss and Howe apply to a rising generation, we can predict that the Net Geners "will rebel against Generation X [pessimistic and selfish] styles and attitudes, correct for Baby Boomer excesses, and fill the [hero] role vacated by the G.I. [Generation]" (2006, 47–48). No small order!

The positive predictions for the Net Generation may come as a surprise. Perceptions of the Net Generation have often been clouded by the less-than-model behavior of Generation X because the delineation between the two is not always clear. In spite of the misconceptions and the media's often negative portrayal, research suggests that Net Geners are actually quite promising.

Rates of violent crime among teens have fallen by 70% in the past ten years, and teen suicide and abortion rates are down, as are reported levels of alcohol and cigarette use and binge drinking (Strauss and Howe 2006, 41). Net Geners are active in the community, as demonstrated by a threefold increase in community service by teens since 1984. This rise in community service is in part explained by a 1999 Roper survey that found that more teenagers blame "selfishness" than anything else when asked about "the major cause of problems in this country" (Strauss and Howe 2006, 42).

In addition to being civic-minded, Net Geners are impressive students. Between 1996 and 2004, the number of high school students who took and passed AP tests increased by 117% among white non-Latinos, 164% among blacks, and 197% among Latinos. Eight in ten say it is cool to be smart (Strauss and Howe 2006, 44). As a group, Net Geners are well on their way to being the best-educated generation in U.S. history.

Defining the Net Generation

Although still in their "formative" period, the Net Geners are beginning to develop some core, shared traits, many of which will have a significant impact on their higher education experiences. Several reports have posited some core traits for Net Geners, including a two-year study of undergraduate students conducted by myself and many of my colleagues at the River Campus Libraries, University of Rochester. The paragraphs that follow focus on some of these emerging core traits for the Net Generation and what they might mean for higher education.

Net Geners have led *sheltered and protected* lives. As Howe and Strauss (2000) explain, this generation is in many ways epitomized by the emergence of those yellow "baby on board" signs in cars. Neighborhood pickup games have been replaced by structured, scheduled playdates. The increased importance of the welfare of children in American society can be seen at both local and national levels with programs such as "No Child Left Behind," stricter movie and television ratings, and a multiplicity of youth advocacy groups. As a consequence of their sheltered childhoods, Net Geners have a strong expectation for secure and regulated environments, with plenty of safety nets, both socially and academically.

Net Geners do not, however, appear to be rebellious toward their parents or resent a childhood marked by intense protection. In fact, more than nine in ten teens say they "trust" and "feel close to their parents" (Strauss and Howe 2006, 42). Relatively speaking, Net Geners are quite *conventional* and appear to share a belief that "social rules and standards make life easier" (Strauss and Howe 2006, 78).

As a result of this close bond and shared conventionalism, the parents of Net Geners have an increased presence, both physical and virtual, on college campuses. This has led to the term "helicopter parents" to describe those who seem to hover over their college-bound children. In our study of undergraduate students, we found the parent presence to be so strong that we completely revamped the libraries' activities during freshman orientation. Instead of preaching to the wide-eyed freshmen about the benefits of the libraries—when clearly those young students were far more interested in finding out about their dorm life, classes, and dining plans—we now focus our orientation activities on their parents. During the 2006 freshman orientation, the libraries hosted a breakfast for parents. While conversing with them, listening to their hopes and fears for their children starting college and helping to dry a few tears, the librarians delivered a simple, concise message: "Every class has a librarian." If the parents retain that message, when their son or daughter calls home for advice and help on a class assignment, perhaps they will suggest that their child make contact with the librarians.

One consequence of this sheltered and protected childhood is that Net Geners have developed a strong sense that they are *special*. The "older generations have inculcated in Millennials the sense that they are, collectively, vital to the nation and to their parents' sense of purpose" (Strauss and Howe 2006, 77). When Net Generation students come to campus, they naturally expect the special treatment to continue. Wager suggests that one manifestation of this attitude is that college "students want customized and personalized services, not a one-size-fits-all approach. There is little question that the Net Generation has expectations that are more encompassing, and perhaps more demanding, than those of previous generations" (2005, 10.5–6). These expectations extend to all parts of campus, including the library. My colleague and lead anthropologist for our undergraduate study, Nancy Fried Foster, uses the term "mommy model of service" as a way of denoting student expectations for service on campus.

Net Geners also have higher levels of *self-esteem* than previous generations. Twenge reports that, by the mid-1990s, the average college male had higher self-esteem than 86% of college men in 1968. For women this number is 71%. This high self-esteem leads to positive, perhaps unrealistic, self-assessments. When asked to describe themselves, 91% of teens described themselves as "responsible," 74% as "physically attractive," and 79% as "very intelligent" (Twenge 2006, 52). These unrealistic self-assessments and overconfidence can lead to great disappointment and defensiveness when reality does not correspond with self-perceptions.

As a generation, Net Geners are markedly both *confident* and *optimistic* (Howe and Strauss 2000; Strauss and Howe 2006). Howe and Strauss found that nine in ten Net Geners would describe themselves as "happy," "confident," and "optimistic" (2000, 7), which is quite a change from their pessimistic Generation X predecessors. They foresee a promising future for both themselves and the country.

Another significant difference from Generation X is the fact that Net Geners are *team oriented*. Throughout their young lives, the importance of teamwork has been regularly enforced. Team sports, group projects, and group "dating" are the norm, and they seem to gravitate naturally toward team activities. Howe and Strauss point to the difference in children's television programming as a manifestation of this changing orientation: "In tot-TV, *Barney and Friends* (with its happy teamwork and stress on what all kids share in common) stole the limelight from *Sesame Street* (with its more nuanced storyline and stress on what makes each kid different)" (2000, 36).

On an academic campus, this means that Net Gener students are not just comfortable working together in groups, they may prefer it, and this can have a significant impact on the types of activities they seek and the facilities needed to support them. For example, as part of our undergraduate study, we asked students to participate in design workshops in which they used poster board, markers, Post-it notes, scissors, and glue to create their ideal library space. The presence of group study areas was one of the most common elements throughout the designs. With designs that included whiteboard, conference tables, and partitions or other structures to provide some level of privacy, the students sent a clear message that they wanted the library to be more than a quiet place for solitary study. Consequently, at the River Campus Libraries the team orientation of students has driven a $5 million renovation to the main campus library to build a 24/7 student collaborative learning center.

In spite of all of their team play, few would describe the childhood of a Net Gener as carefree. Instead, *pressured* is a much more appropriate characterization. Net Geners feel tremendous pressure, from their parents and collectively from society, to take full advantage of all of the available opportunities afforded them. On the positive side, this means that Net Geners are "on track to becoming the smartest, best-educated generation of adults in U.S. history" (Strauss and Howe 2006, 78). On the negative side, Net Geners are experiencing many more emotional disorders than previous generations. A 1990s study discovered that 21% of teens between the ages of 15 and 17 had already experienced an episode of major depression (Twenge 2006, 105).

Similarly, anxiety among college students is on the rise. Twenge found that "anxiety increased so much that the average college student in the 1990s was more anxious than 85% of students in the 1950s and 71% of students in the 1970s." She was also able to show that when you were born has more influence on anxiety than your family environment, with "generational differences accounting for 20% of the variation in anxiety" (2006, 107).

The pressure to achieve has meant that Net Geners' lives are quite regulated and focused. Between 1981 and 1997, "free" or "unsupervised" time in the daily lives of American preteens dropped by 37% (Howe and Strauss 2000, 9). By the time they come to campus, Net Geners have internalized the pressure to achieve, and consequently they want to know explicitly what the rules are to succeed (Oblinger and Oblinger 2005)—what exactly it is going to take to get an A in this or that class.

A common question we asked students in our undergraduate study was how they kept track of their time. The mechanisms varied from PDAs to paper date calendars to innumerable Post-it notes, but there was a lot of similarity. Students had their days planned, often to the minute, with few unscheduled blocks of time. From the time they woke, these students were constantly on the move between classes, group study, part-time jobs, meetings with professors and classmates, student organization meetings, trips to the gym, extra hours in the lab, and an occasional social event. Looking at these schedules, one would have to assume that college is no longer a period of personal freedom, isolated from the pace and stress of the "real world" that awaits after graduation.

In an effort to achieve all that is expected of them, Net Geners have become skilled as *multitaskers*. They seem to be able to juggle many tasks at once effortlessly, such as writing a paper, having one or more conversations via instant message, listening to music, and watching a television program. This coping strategy, coined "continuous partial attention" by Linda Stone of Microsoft Research, can seem a dizzying feat to many. The numerous tasks undertaken simultaneously are, however, not necessarily accomplished equally well. For Net Geners, "more value [is] placed on speed than on accuracy" (Oblinger and Oblinger 2005, 26). Time appears to be the scarcest resource in a Net Generation student's life.

As one would expect from a generation that has grown up on music and computer videos, Net Geners are both *digitally and visually literate* (Oblinger and Oblinger 2005). They are attuned to visual messages and have fine-tuned visual-spatial skills. As a consequence of their digital and visual literacy, they often seek these mediums for expression and communication.

To a degree many might find shocking, Net Geners are emotionally *very open*. Online blogs and social networking sites such as Facebook and MySpace are full of intimate, personal details including emotional problems, drug abuse, and sexual exploits. As Twenge discovered when she asked her students to write true stories as part of a class assignment, "none of the students cared if I knew details of their personal lives that other generations would have kept as carefully guarded secrets" (2006, 36). For Net Geners, there appears to be little that would fall into the category of "too much information," with 62% of 18- to 24-year-olds indicating that they are comfortable discussing their personal problems with others. For those age 65 and older, that number falls to only 37% (Twenge 2006, 37).

Above all, the way the Net Generation differs the most from the preceding generations is in its use, comfort, and familiarity with digital technology, and it is here that the generation gap is felt most clearly.

The Net Generation Gap

Generation gaps are as old as humankind. Each generation is unique by "acquiring a shared history that lends its members a social and cultural center of gravity" (Strauss and Howe 2006, 20). For the Net Generation, it is digital technology that resides at the social and cultural center. Net Geners are the first to have spent their entire lives engaging digital technology. They have been referred to as "digital natives" because they are all "native speakers" of the digital language of computers, video games, and the Internet (Prensky 2001, 1). Although the Internet and digital technologies have touched all of our lives in some way, most librarians, particularly those in the greatest positions of authority, are "digital immigrants." "As Digital Immigrants learn . . . to adapt to their environment, they always retain, to some degree, their 'accent' that is their foot in the past" (Prensky 2001, 2). Consequently, no matter how fluent and comfortable we become with digital technology, we will always retain something of our "analog" background.

The distinction between digital immigrant and native manifests itself in fundamental differences between the Net Generation and those who came before. Tapscott (1997, 48–50) points to three major factors that have opened up this generational abyss: (1) The older generations are uneasy about the new technology—which kids are embracing; (2) older generations tend to be uneasy about new media—which are coming into the heart of youth culture; and (3) the digital revolution, unlike previous ones, is not controlled by only adults.

"To a great extent, the behaviors of the Net Gen are an enactment of the capabilities afforded by modern digital technologies" (Hartman, Moskal, and Dziuban 2005, 6.3), and those capabilities continue to expand at an astonishing pace. Technology abounds in the lives of Net Geners, and when they come to campus their technology comes with them. A 2005 ECAR report revealed that

93.4% of college students owned a computer. Seventy percent of college seniors owned a desktop computer and 38.5% a laptop. For freshmen, those numbers were 57.1% and 52.7% (some students have both), respectively, which indicates a rather rapid shift away from desktops to laptop computers. Cell phones are another popular technology coming to campus, with 84.7% of female and 77.7% of male students bringing them in 2005 (Caruso and Kvavik 2005, 13).

The technology students bring to campus is, in the students' mind, not in fact technology. As Oblinger and Oblinger explain, Net Geners "don't think in terms of technology; they think in terms of the activity technology enables" (2005, 2.10). Moreover, for Net Geners "the definition of technology is not confined to computers or the Internet. Technology is viewed as any electronically based application or piece of equipment that meets a need for access to information or communication" (Roberts 2005, 3.2). Much of this activity centers on networking and socializing. Communication and social activities are rapidly moving online, via instant messaging, e-mail, cell phones, and text messaging. It is, however, important not to interpret this to mean that Net Geners are less social or that their personal relationships are shallower. Rather, the use of technology actually deepens the relationships by providing ways for friends to remain nearly constantly in touch throughout the day. In other words, the use of instant messaging, text messaging, and the rest is supplemental to the "real," human-to-human connections that are made.

Net Geners are quite confident in their ability to use technology. In general, they self-report high skill levels for e-mail, instant messaging, word processing, and web surfing (Kvavik 2005, 7.5). Their confidence does not, however, spread across all technologies. Lower self-assessment of skills is reported for using graphics software, creating web pages with programs such as Dreamweaver and FrontPage, and creating and editing video and audio files (Kvavik 2005, 7.6). It is interesting to note that "online library resources" reside right in the middle of the range, suggesting that there is still work to be done to make students more comfortable with online library resources and thereby increase their self-assessed library skills. (See table 2-1.)

Students believe technology should be part of their academic life, not just their social life. When asked what benefits information technology can bring to a class, 48% of students responded with "convenience" as their top choice, followed by "helped me manage my class activities" and "saved me time" (Kvavik 2005, 7.13).

Net Geners are able to move seamlessly between physical and virtual interactions (Oblinger and Oblinger 2005) and are weaving technology into their lives, both inside and outside the classroom. This in turn is leading to new academic and social norms (Hartman, Moskal, and Dziuban 2005, 6.1).

TABLE 2-1
Skill levels attained

Application	Mean[a]	Std. deviation
E-mail	3.60	0.525
Instant messenger	3.54	0.652
Word processing	3.53	0.553
Web surfing	3.47	0.578
Presentation software (PowerPoint, etc.)	2.90	0.762
Online library resources	2.88	0.687
Spreadsheets (Excel, etc.)	2.86	0.763
Course management systems	2.83	0.744
Graphics (Photoshop, Flash, etc.)	2.45	0.846
Creating web pages (Dreamweaver, FrontPage, etc.)	2.17	0.910
Creating and editing video/audio (Director, iMovie, etc.)	2.07	0.848

Source: Reproduced with permission from Kvavik, Caruso, and Morgan (2004, 5).

[a] Scale = 1 (very unskilled) to 4 (very skilled)

However, as Hartman, Moskal and Dziuban explain, Net Generation students' "rapid adoption of instant messaging, cell phones, blogs, wikis, social networking Web sites, and other resources that are not generally part of the core campus infrastructure leads to a host of new concerns" (2005, 6.5). These concerns include issues of security, copyright infringement, and the costs of bandwidth, data storage, and wireless campuses, but they also involve the academy's and library's ability to integrate these new technologies and their accompanying academic and social norms into the existing infrastructure, services, digital environment, and physical facilities.

Put simply, the Net Generation does things differently. They communicate differently (e.g., text messaging and instant messaging). They use a different written language (with phrases like "lol," "cya," and "l8r"). They interact and socialize differently (e.g., via avatars in online games and Facebook). They have a different sense of authorship (e.g., Flickr and personal blogs). And most important in the context of academic libraries, Net Geners' "affinity for technology translates into new and different expectations about how to gather, work with, translate, and share information" (Rainie 2006, 3). In the following chapters we explore how the Net Generation, as the first generation of digital natives, uses different kinds of technology and why, and what impact this should have on the future of academic libraries.

CHAPTER THREE

Online Gaming

THERE ARE A MULTIPLICITY OF WAYS BY WHICH generations can be defined and identified. The flapper-style dress defines the 1920s in much the same way tie-dye and bell-bottoms epitomized the 1960s and the Baby Boomers. Similarly, the Ford Thunderbird is emblematic of the late 1950s and 1960s, whereas minivans and sport utility vehicles are the choice for growing families of the Generation Xers. Another way to define a generation is by the games it plays; in the case of the Net Generation, its games offer great insight into how academic libraries could be recasting and realigning themselves with the social and academic practices of students.

In the 1930s, the G.I. Generation was playing pinball, Scrabble, and Monopoly; games such as Twister, Stratego, and Risk were all the rage with the Boomers. Generation X saw the introduction of early computer games, including Pong and Space Invaders, as well as the widely popular Dungeons and Dragons dice and role-playing game. As the Generation Xers entered high school and college, they began playing Pac-Man, Tetris, and Trivial Pursuit and then in the 1990s turned to elaborate computer games such as Civilization, Myst, and Grand Theft Auto (Svaboda 2006, 132). Today's Net Generation will, however, likely be remembered best for MMORPGs, the acronym for "massive, multiplayer, online role-playing games."

There are many genres of computer games, and these range widely in complexity, cost, and degree of interactivity. Small handheld game devices such as Game Boys are popular for their great portability. "Console games," on the other hand, require specialized, dedicated hardware, such as the Microsoft Xbox, Sony PlayStation, and Nintendo GameCube, which are connected to a television screen. Laptop and desktop computers can also be used as gaming platforms, which come in the form of software that can be played on the computer without any additional hardware. Examples of these games range from the ubiquitous Solitaire and Mine Sweeper to the complex, highly immersive games of Electronic Arts' Sims series and Microsoft's Flight Simulator. In addition, the computer can serve as a gateway to games on the Internet, with no additional software needed. These include free, single-player games, such as those found on MSN Games, or games played by physically dispersed players, including Texas Holdem Poker and Hearts.[1] At the far end of the current spectrum of online games are MMORPGs.

MMORPGs are online computer games that are highly graphic and incredibly immersive. The games take place in 2-D or 3-D online worlds that tend to have a medieval, fantasy, or alien theme. The game itself runs on a server or servers somewhere in the world. Players load specific software onto their personal computers, through which they can connect to the game server, via the Internet, and play the game. In the United States the game software can cost around $50, with an additional $10–$15 monthly subscription fee (Castronova 2005, 52). What makes MMORPGs so different from past online games is that they can be played by hundreds, often thousands, of people worldwide, simultaneously. The game is always "on," with activity occurring continuously, 24/7.

As a player, you are represented in the game by a digital character, called an avatar. Your avatar is usually highly personalized. You can determine your own hair, skin, and eye coloring, craft a body shape and type to your liking, select your gender, and even choose your species: human, ogre, elf, Star Wars Wookiee. Once you have crafted your avatar, it serves as your representation within the game and acts as a sort of proxy as you converse, fight, work, and play with other players' avatars in the virtual world.

When avatars are in the same relative proximity within the virtual game world, they can interact by online chat or voice over IP (VoIP) and through a wide spectrum of gestures. Although the games have a loosely structured narrative that provides some organization to the activities, such as quests, they contain ample unregulated opportunities to socialize and be creative. At any given moment players may be participating in comedy nights, amateur theatricals, marriages, funerals, pet shows, and disco parties or just sitting at the edge of a serene lake virtually fishing (Kolbert 2001, 88).

To get a feel for the scope and depth of these virtual interactions, view one of the "cantina crawls" from the MMORPG Star Wars Galaxy (Cantina Crawl VII is a personal favorite).[2] These are elaborately choreographed music videos, but, unlike those on MTV, these music videos take place in virtual locations and the dancers are virtual avatars. (See fig. 3-1.) Behind these performances are the carefully choreographed, simultaneous keystrokes of hundreds of people from around the world. Social, communal activities like the cantina

FIGURE 3-1
Scene from Cantina Crawl VII from the online game Star Wars Galaxy

crawls have little if anything to do with the overall objectives of the game itself. Rather, they are manifestations of the innate human desire to interact with others, even if it is through the proxy of an avatar.

In many ways, the activities in a MMORPG mirror the trials and tribulations of the real world, in what Kolbert refers to as a "perversely recurrent social realism" (2001, 88). When studying one of the earliest MMORPGs, Ultima Online, she found prostitution, hoarding, counterfeiting, murder, and numerous other forms of unseemly activities. It seems that even in virtual worlds social problems exist.

Show Me the Numbers

If you are new to the concept of MMORPGs, you may find the user numbers and demographics quite surprising. In 2005, 81% of teen Internet users in the United States—that's 17 million of them—played online games. Even more impressive is the fact that this number has increased by 52% since 2000 (Lenhart, Madden, and Hitlin 2005, i). Although it is difficult to calculate precise figures, Bruce Woodcock, an independent analyzer of online gaming, regularly provides

some well-grounded estimates on his website for MMORPG gamers (www
.mmogchart.com). In June 2006, Woodcock identified twelve MMORPGs with
120,000 or more subscribers worldwide, with three of the games exceeding one
million subscribers (Woodcock 2006): Lineage (1.5 million subscribers) and
Lineage II (1.3 million subscribers) are medieval worlds with dragons to slay
and castles to siege. World of Warcraft, created by Blizzard Entertainment,
currently exceeds all other games in popularity, claiming an astounding 6.5
million subscribers in its fantasy world of quests.

The activities within a virtual game rarely stay bound by the game. Accompanying MMORPGs are real-time conferences and official and unofficial
game websites, which provide guides, blogs, news, support, and downloads.
Economic activity also spills over the virtual borders. Edward Castronova, an
economics professor at Indiana University, has focused his research on the
economic aspects of online games, which he refers to as "synthetic worlds."
In particular, Castronova studies "the extent to which people are paying real
money to buy items for their game characters, thus blurring the distinction
between the game economy and the real one."[3] Although certainly not a
traditional field of economic study, it is one that recently has received a great
deal of attention and press.

While playing EverQuest, a popular MMORPG, Castronova noticed that
economic transactions were an important aspect of the game world. Not only
were avatars exchanging information and virtual objects for game money, but
real money was exchanging hands as well. Using online auction sites such
as eBay, players auction off virtual money and objects for real currencies
(Castronova 2005, 149). For example, on June 6, 2006, an auction on eBay closed
for three EverQuest accounts. The virtual items were listed as "3 everquest
accounts 70necro+ 67sk/50sham+ 35sk/68mag" and had a starting bid of $200
and a "Buy It Now" price of $1,000. What was actually for sale were three
EverQuest accounts with their respective avatars and the accumulated wealth
and skills of each. The numbers refer to the skill level of the avatars, and the
letters indicate the characters' class, such as necromancer, shadow knight,
shaman, or magician.

By studying economic transactions such as this, Castronova was able to
conclude that within the EverQuest world called Norrath the hourly wage was
about US$3.42, with a gross national product per capita of "somewhere between
that of Russia and Bulgaria." If the Norrath currency could be traded on foreign
exchange markets, it would have a value of approximately $0.0107, which in
2001 was higher than the Japanese yen and Italian lira (Castronova 2001, 1, 3).

With more than $2 billion in subscription revenues in 2005 and the
millions of dollars spent on virtual items and services outside the games,

MMORPGs cannot be easily ignored as an insignificant, merely entertaining pastime. Rather, they are being taken seriously as forms of communication, socialization, education, and even business. This is further indicated by the appearance of an article on avatar-based marketing in the June 2006 issue of the prestigious *Harvard Business Review* (Hemp 2006). Online games are rapidly becoming mainstream.

Who Are These Gamers?

The demographics of online gamers are as surprising as the economics. The stereotype of an online gamer is of an antisocial teenage male, playing endless hours of computer games, alone. The growing body of demographic studies of online gamers, however, indicates something quite different. The most expansive collection of quantitative and qualitative gamer data to date was collected by Nick Yee, a doctoral student in Stanford University's department of communication. Over a period of five years, Yee (2001b) collected online survey results from more than 35,000 MMORPG players. He found that 85% of MMORPG players are male. This is consistent with Laber's estimate that 20–30% of the players of the games Ultima Online, Asheron's Call, and EverQuest are women (2001, G1). On the other hand, when players of all types of computer games, including "casual games" such as Solitaire and Tetris, are included, women outnumber men by two to one (Brightman 2006).

A MMORPG player is not limited to a single avatar. She can have more than one avatar associated with her account, each with different characteristics. This flexibility facilitates the interesting phenomenon of virtual gender switching. In EverQuest, Yee found that 47.9% of men and 23.3% of women reported owning an avatar of the opposite gender. The reasons given for this gender bending include "gender exploration," "visual appearance," and "for role play purposes" (2001a).

Players of all types of computer games, including MMORPGs, are older than most people would guess. Yee found that the average age of MMORPG gamers is 26.6 years. When broken down by gender, the average age for women is 31.72 years, with 25.71 years for men (2001b). A study of EverQuest players found similar results, with 66% of users being between the ages of 21 and 40 (Griffiths, Davies, and Chappell 2003, 84). In sum, although the male stereotype is correct, at least for MMORPGs, only about 25% of players are teenagers (Yee 2001b).

Another misconception of online gamers is that they are antisocial. Of EverQuest players, 36% were found to be married and 22% had children (Yee 2001b). MMORPG players are actively engaged with the nonvirtual world, with

50% working full-time and another 22% busy as full-time students. Moreover, Yee discovered that it was quite common for players to engage in the games with real-life acquaintances. Of female players, 60% reported playing with a romantic partner and 40% played with a family member. For male players, these numbers drop to 16% and 26%, respectively (Yee 2001a).

As part of a larger study of online games, Taylor mapped out the relationships she found in a group of twenty gamers who formed a guild in EverQuest. In that guild were five married couples, five off-line friends, two brothers, and two cousins. The guild also contained several virtual relationships, including two virtually married couples and a virtual mother/daughter pair (2006, 55). As Taylor concludes, MMORPGs are "by their very nature social ventures in that they involve numerous players gaming together in real time in a shared virtual environment" (2006, 36). The medium of online games can obscure the reality that, behind the avatars and virtual landscapes, there are humans with an innate desire to socialize.

The social nature of MMORPGs is more than a side attraction. In fact, many games are designed such that "success" is dependent on the ability to collaborate and coordinate efforts with other players. For example, Steinkuehler describes the medieval world of Lineage, where the characters with the most positional authority, princes and princesses, must protect their castles from siege by forming a series of alliances, or blood pledges, with other, more combat-ready characters (2004, 521). The Lineage player website explains that the concept of a blood pledge "will be the ideals of friendship, family, and community, united together to achieve a common goal."[4] Consequently, large-scale cooperation and collaboration with other players is required in order to succeed in most games, thus making traits such as "fun to be with" and "plays well with others" advantageous for a serious gamer.

The average amount of time spent playing MMORPGs is at first glance rather high. One study found that 26.2% of MMORPG gamers played 1–10 hours per week, 32.6% played 10–20 hours, and 21.2% played 20–30 hours (Yee 2004, 1). But these numbers do not seem so high when compared with other forms of media use. For example, one way to understand the increasing time spent playing online games is to weigh it against the dropping number of hours of television watching. In 1999, television watching made up 39% of the total time spent with media by children and young adults between the ages of 8 and 18. Five years later this number had dropped to 34%. In the same period, however, the combination of computer and video game use rose from 12% to 20% (Strauss and Howe 2006, 205). In other words, some gamers have exchanged their passive hours of television watching for interactive hours of online game playing.

A recent survey of MIT freshmen found that 88% began playing computer games before they were 10 years old, and more than 75% currently played at least once a month. Of those MIT freshmen, 60% spent an hour or more playing computer games each week, but only 33% reported spending that much time watching television (Squire and Jenkins 2003, 11).

As Yee (2001b) points out, "MMORPGs are a very unique environment, in that you would almost never, in real life, find high-school students, housewives, retirees and early adult professionals together in any sort of collaborative decision-making task." In spite of the stereotype of young antisocial men, MMORPGs actually embrace a stunningly wide, demographically diverse cross section of the world's population.

The Appeal of Online Games

So what is it about online games, and MMORPGs in particular, that makes them so appealing to such large numbers of people across such a wide spectrum of demographics? This question is starting to attract a great deal of attention, fostering many hypotheses. Johnson suggests that it is the continuous promise of rewards that makes the game world so captivating and attractive. "If you create a system where rewards are both clearly defined and achieved by exploring the environment, you'll find human brains drawn to those systems, even if they're made up of virtual characters and simulated sidewalks" (2005, 38).

Gee (2005) explains the appeal of computer games in a similar fashion: "Each level dances around the outer limits of the player's abilities, seeking at every point to be hard enough to be just doable." The innate human desire for rewards is carefully leveraged by online games to ensure that rewards are difficult to obtain but not so challenging as to cause immense frustration. In other words, a reward is always just within reach.

Steinkuehler (2005) describes the attraction of MMORPGs by using Oldenburg's concept of the "third place"—"public places on neutral ground where people can gather and interact. In contrast to first places (home) and second places (work), third places allow people to put aside their concerns and simply enjoy the company and conversation around them."[5] Starbucks, German beer gardens, French cafés, and the local English pub are all examples of popular third places, and Steinkuehler observes that MMORPGs are an emerging class of third places as well.

One characteristic of a third place is that it is on "neutral ground." Third places are where "individuals may come and go as they please, in which none are required to play host, and in which all feel at home and comfortable"

(Oldenburg 1999, 22). MMORPGs certainly fit this description. So long as a player has paid his subscription fees, he is free to enter and leave the games at any temporal point. He can engage in the game in a completely anonymous state, through his avatar, and can determine if and when to reveal personal details. As Steinkuehler and Williams (2006) note, "These avatars bear no relationship to one's offline identity, unless one chooses to render one's own character so identifiable. . . . [T]his anonymity provides a safe haven beyond the reach of work and home that allows individuals to engage with others without entangling obligations and repercussions." The decision to create a new avatar, leave a particular guild, or move to a different game and virtual world always rests completely within the player's control.

A second quality of third places is that they are societal levelers. They are "accessible to the general public and [do] not set formal criteria of membership and exclusion" (Oldenburg 1999, 24). An appealing aspect of playing online games is that they are incredibly democratizing. In a MMORPG, what matters and is valued are experience and knowledge of the game, regardless of one's status in the real world. As Steinkuehler explains, "Acceptance and participation are not contingent on any prerequisites, requirements, roles, duties, or proof of membership" (2005, 22). A player's true age, race, gender, class, and nationality have no meaning in the virtual world. Nor does wealth, educational level, or physical appearance (Squire and Steinkuehler 2005, 38).

Status is equally available to all through game expertise, which is acquired primarily by spending time playing the game. Some gamers have found this to be quite liberating. For example, in studying the attraction of MMORPGs to women, Taylor noted the freedom afforded by casting off the limitations of one's gender:

> Unlike the real world in which gender often plays a significant role in not only the perception of one's safety, but its actuality, in EverQuest women may travel [virtually] knowing they are no more threatened by the creatures of the world than their male counterparts are. (2003, 32)

MMORPGs ignore all the usual categories that stratify society and give all players an equal chance for success and reward.

In MMORPGs, as in other third places, conversations are the main activity. The 3-D gaming worlds are awash in conversations, which form the foundation for successful play. In Lineage II, Steinkuehler found numerous kinds of conversations:

> Multiple conversations occur in tandem with individuals oftentimes engaged in several conversational threads simultaneously—sharing a laugh over clan

chat about someone's recent untimely online death, haggling over the price of some sorely needed item on trade chat, arguing in party chat about how to distribute the spoils of the hunting groups' current escapade, privately catching up through private whispered talk with a good friend who had been offline the day before. (2005, 25)

Successful game play is dependent upon the ability to build online relationships, which grow from the many types of conversations that can occur.

Another characteristic of a good third place is that it is both accessible and accommodating. Oldenburg explains that "access to them must be *easy* . . . and the ease with which one may visit a third place is both a matter of time and location" (1999, 32). Consequently, the most successful third places are open long hours and are in locations that are easy to reach. Regardless of the time of day, online games are always on, and there are always players to engage. The games have no temporal or geographic boundaries, thereby permitting people from across the world an opportunity to meet, communicate, exchange ideas, and hang out together. For those people who enjoy socializing, the possibilities for new social relations in online games are nearly inexhaustible.

The constant presence of "regulars" is another characteristic of third places. It is the regulars "who give the place its character and who assure that on any given visit some of the gang will be there" (Oldenburg 1999, 34). In Lineage II, Steinkuehler determined that it was fellow clan members who became the regulars, who "set the tone of sociability by remaining ever-present within the clan chat window" (2005, 26). In addition to one's clan mates, there are regulars who Steinkuehler and Williams (2006) refer to as "squatters." These are players who tend to reside in specific virtual locations, "providing a social context specific to the various areas in the game." For example, some virtual areas within Lineage II are known for the type of raunchy banter and commentary engaged in by the regulars.

Oldenburg also describes the third place as a "home away from home," where people feel rooted and have a sense of possession and control "that need not entail actual ownership" (1999, 40). Steinkuehler found these same homey aspects in Lineage II. After a three-day absence from the game, her return was met by inquiries from fellow clan members about her unannounced absence, with one 14-year-old advising her, "Next time, just let us know in advance" (2005, 28). Within a MMORPG, fellow players "create an atmosphere of mutual caring that, while avoiding entangling obligations per se, creates a sense of rootedness to the extent that regularities exist, irregularities are duly noted, and, when concerning the welfare of any one regular [gamer], checked into" (Steinkuehler and Williams 2006).

The appeal of online games can be difficult to recognize and discern by nongamers. As hard as it can sometimes be to imagine, the world of online games is far from solitary. It is a place where all are welcome to come and go as they please, with the assurance that someone will always be there to keep them company. MMORPGs have succeeded in creating virtual environments that are intellectually challenging but still socially welcoming. They are places where people from the entire world can interact, collaborate, and engage, free from the undertones of differences in race, gender, religion, age, and socioeconomic status. Can any physical place claim as much?

Educational Benefits of Gaming

Whenever the benefits of computer games are debated, physiological improvements invariably top the list—and these are not only matters of increased hand-eye coordination. A recent study at the University of Rochester found that video game playing is "capable of radically altering visual attention processing" (Green and Bavelier 2003, 536) in ways that improve the ability to keep track of objects that appear simultaneously and to process changing visual information faster (Associated Press 2003). A remarkable finding in this study is that it took a mere ten days of video game playing for attention-processing changes to become detectable.

The benefits of online games go beyond physiological improvement as well. When games are designed well they can be powerful learning tools, which can be explained through the lenses of several learning theories. Both Dede (2005) and Gee (2003) explain the learning potential of video games with theories of situated meaning and learning. Learning can be much more effective when the learner has the opportunity to experiment, practice, and apply the newly acquired understanding immediately. When playing a well-designed game, the player engages in the following steps:

1. The player must *probe* the virtual world by moving through the virtual environment and clicking on the objects within.
2. Based on the information gathered from this probing, the player forms a *hypothesis* about what something might mean.
3. The player then *reprobes* the game with the hypothesis in mind, experimenting to see if the hypothesis is correct.
4. Based on the feedback, the player will accept or rethink the hypothesis (Gee 2003, 90).

This process may seem familiar, for it is the basis of scientific inquiry and method. In other words, a well-designed video or online game is actually an opportunity for players to internalize the process of scientific inquiry.

Van Eck has suggested that the learning theories of Jean Piaget can also shed light on the learning benefits of gaming (2006, 18–20). Piaget described learning as the result of a cycle of assimilation, cognitive disequilibrium, and accommodation. When a person acquires some new bit of information, he tries to fit, or assimilate, it with his existing knowledge and understanding. There are, however, times when new information contradicts preexisting understandings or beliefs, which causes a cognitive disequilibrium. Since a person cannot hold two contradictory beliefs, he must change his existing model or understanding in order to accommodate this new information. Well-designed online games "embody this process of cognitive disequilibrium and resolution" (Van Eck 2006, 16). For example, a rash of faculty resignations within the game Virtual U (www.virtual-u.org) should cause you, as president of the virtual university, to reconsider your hypothesis about the relationship between starting a summer session and faculty morale.

Another way to frame the potential learning of playing an online game is as a clever "bait and switch." Although gamers may be playing for the entertainment value, "virtual worlds facilitate 'unintentional' learning, where students discover and create knowledge not for its own sake but in order to accomplish something they want to do, resulting in stronger comprehension and deeper knowledge" (EDUCAUSE Learning Initiative 2006). Becoming familiar with the events of the American Civil War may not be one's intention as they begin to play the game American Civil War: Gettysburg, but it is a consequence nonetheless.

More than one opponent of gaming has pitted computer gaming against reading: "My kids don't play computer games, they read." What is often overlooked is the fact that gaming can actually encourage reading. When Squire and Steinkuehler meet with students, they always ask if anyone has checked out a book from the library based on an interest generated through game play. Their unscientific survey found that about half of the students had. The percentage is nearly 100% for those students who played more historically based games, such as Age of Empires, Civilization, and Rome: Total War. "Games such as these could be one of the best untapped links to books for librarians: they require serious thought and stimulate an interest in multiple topics including history, politics, economics, and geography" (Squire and Steinkuehler 2005, 38).

The highly graphic aspects of an online game often overshadow the more traditional forms of literacy required for successful playing. In studying Lineage, Squire and Steinkuehler discovered a continual need for reading, writing, and the assimilation and synthesis of text. For example, to conduct sieges and defend castles successfully, players engage in activities such as researching equipment, managing resources, drawing maps, investing money, building models, designing strategies, and debating facts and theories (2005, 38). Consequently, these research skills are important to the game as a source of prestige and to provide a competitive edge.

Educational Gaming

There is a growing corpus of games specifically designed for educational purposes as well as commercial games that contain educational content. A collaboration between MIT and the University of Wisconsin known as the Education Arcade (educationarcade.org) is designing games with deliberate educational goals. Under development is Revolution, a MMORPG based on the historical events of colonial Williamsburg, Virginia. Students can role-play in any of seven classes of characters, including an upper-class lawyer and an African American house slave. Environmental Detectives is an outdoor game in which players use GPS-guided handheld computers to uncover the source of a virtual toxic spill. MIT Ghost will create a persistent online representation of MIT that is intended to make "MIT cultures more widely accessible, especially to potential applicants and incoming students." Imagine how much easier your freshman year would have been had you had the opportunity to explore all of campus and meet classmates virtually before the start of classes.

Another MIT gaming partnership is with the Royal Shakespeare Company. Together they are developing Prospero's Island as a "gateway" into Shakespeare's *Tempest:*

> The game is not simply a literal-minded adaptation of Shakespeare's play; it doesn't simply play out the plot with limited roles for player intervention. Rather, the game is a deconstruction or interpretation of the play as rich and original as the [Royal Shakespeare Company's] provocative stage performances. (Squire and Jenkins 2003, 20)

Collaboration between Harvard University and Arizona State University, with funding from the National Science Foundation, has led to the development of River City, which provides an immersive platform for the study of biology and epidemiology:

> As visitors to River City, students travel back in time, bringing their 21st century skills and technology to address 19th century problems. River City is a town besieged with health problems. Students work together in small research teams to help the town understand why so many residents are

becoming ill. Students use technology to keep track of clues that hint at causes of illnesses, form and test hypotheses, develop controlled experiments to test their hypotheses, and make recommendations based on the data they collect, all in an online environment.[6]

Dartmouth College has built a simulation of a mass casualty incident to help train emergency responders (McGrath and Hill 2004), and the University of British Columbia created a virtual world of real archaeological sites (EDUCAUSE Learning Initiative 2006). Under the guidance of Edward Castronova, Indiana University is building Arden: The World of William Shakespeare, which "will provide users with a fun experience that also immerses them in the narrative, language, and culture of the world's greatest writer."[7]

Some online games have been developed for both education and political action. MTV Networks recently released Darfur Is Dying (www.darfurisdying .com). As the website describes it, this online game is a "narrative-based simulation where the user, from the perspective of a displaced Darfurian, negotiates forces that threaten the survival of his or her refugee camp. It offers a faint glimpse of what it's like for the more than 2.5 million who have been internally displaced by the crisis in Sudan." Players of Darfur Is Dying are expected to be moved into political action as a consequence of playing the game.

Far more in number are commercial games with strong educational components. The teaching of history can be productively accompanied by the playing of computer games such as Rise of Nations and American Civil War: Gettysburg. Squire (in press) argues for the use of the game Civilization III as a constructive pedagogical tool for "allowing students to understand the positionality and theoretical assumptions behind any representation of history." A few rounds of Roller Coaster Tycoon are being used in an introductory physical science course at the University of Delaware to teach concepts of motion, force, and mechanical energy.[8] The course "Marketing Environment of Management" at the University of Sioux Falls' business school includes playing a round of the economics-based game Lemonade Stand.[9]

If you are still unconvinced of the potential value in online gaming, consider this analogy offered by Will Wright, the creator of the popular Sims game series:

> Imagine that all you know about movies was gleaned through observing the audience in a theater—but that you had never watched a film. You would conclude that movies induce lethargy and junk-food binges. That may be true, but you're missing the big picture. (2006, 111)

It is also helpful to consider gaming in its historical context. Many of the objections and derogatory assumptions currently applied to computer games were once applied to entertainment elements that are commonplace today. Standage invites critics of online games to consider the following possible precedents. In the late 1700s, parents were warned to protect their children from the many dangers of free access to "romances, novels, and plays [which] poisoned the mind and corrupted the morals of many a promising youth" (Reverend Enos Hitchcock, *Memoirs of the Bloomsgrove Family*, quoted in Standage 2006, 114). The early twentieth century witnessed the scourge of "moving pictures" because of which "God alone knows how many are leading dissolute lives" (from *The Annual Report of the New York Society for the Prevention of Cruelty to Children*, quoted in Standage 2006, 114). Or how about the evils of the telephone, which causes laziness, the tendency for crime caused by reading comic books, or the sins of the waltz, with its "voluptuous intertwining of the limbs, and close compressure of the bodies" (from *Times of London*, 1816, quoted in Standage 2006, 114). The pattern is clear: the new form of entertainment of the younger generation is misunderstood and portrayed as the "scourge of society" by the preceding generations.

Brown suggests that many of us miss the importance of online gaming because we focus too tightly on the game itself: "So don't just think about the games themselves—the content—but about the knowledge ecologies developing around these games—the context" (2002, 64). The knowledge ecologies of online games include conversations, reading, writing, research, buying and selling, the formation and dissolution of partnerships and pacts, mentoring, instruction, and a host of other activities. The games do little more than provide a compelling and immersive platform for all of these social activities to occur.

Academic Libraries and Online Gaming

So how can academic libraries respond to the rise in interest in online gaming? There is a wide spectrum of responses, ranging from minor adjustments to a full embrace of the gaming culture.

Virtual Worlds

For those not interested in engaging students in a virtual world fraught with virtual dangers, there are alternative, gameless virtual worlds. Two examples are Second Life (secondlife.com) and Active Worlds (www.activeworlds.com). Both are 3-D virtual worlds, but there are no games associated with them.

Instead, people gather in the worlds, via personal avatars, to talk, debate, enjoy lectures and concerts, and experience the pleasures of designing buildings, gardens, art, and the like.

The virtual world of Second Life (SL) is a self-described "3D online digital world imagined, created, and owned by its residents." Membership to SL comes in two tiers. The first, basic membership, is absolutely free. With it you can create an avatar, participate in the SL events, and wander through the world. The second, the premium account, ranges in price from $9.95 per month to $72.00 for a one-year account. The most desirable privileges that accompany a premium account are the ability to own land and build upon that land. Just as in the physical world, SL land is bought and sold. At the end of November 2006, a U.S. dollar could purchase around 269 Linden dollars, the currency of SL.

Since its public launch in 2003, SL's population has grown to more than 1.67 million members. One of the regions of SL is Info World, where information and knowledge are at the heart of all activities. Currently residing in Info World is the Second Life Library 2.0. (See fig. 3-2.) Coordinated and managed by the Alliance Library System (www.alliancelibrarysystem.com), a group of self-selecting volunteer librarians run the virtual library. In the virtual "main library" resides the reference desk, staffed by avatars, and a virtual computer lab. Nearby is Parvenu Towers, an elegant, ten-story library. Each floor is dedicated to a broad subject area, such as Fine Arts (first floor), Government Documents (second floor), and Science and Technology (fifth floor). Virtual computer terminals that reside on each floor link to real, relevant websites. (See fig. 3-3.) Other libraries in SL include the Mystery Mansion, the Sci-Fi Portal (developed by Talis Information), the Caledon 19th Century Library (avatars must dress in nineteenth-century costumes), a medical library, and the Information and Communications Technology Library.

Essentially, the Second Life Library is positioning itself to support the information needs of the avatars of SL in the same way that a public library seeks to support the information needs of its community. In addition to its reference desk and virtual collections, the Second Life Library hosts programs including book discussions, podcasts, lectures, and even library instruction sessions. You can follow the events and development of the Second Life Library at its blog: infoisland.org.

A second, older virtual world is Active Worlds, where Mark Puterbaugh of Eastern University's library has been creating his Virtual Bibliographic Instruction (VBI) world since 1998. The VBI library is a 3-D virtual building where students can come to ask questions at the reference desk, socialize with friends in virtual rooms, and search for resources in the online catalog and databases (Hawkins and Brynko 2006, 1).

FIGURE 3-2
Alliance Library System's Second Life Library 2.0

FIGURE 3-3
Inside the Second Life Library 2.0

Although Second Life and Active Worlds may seem to be fringe activities, the higher education community's formal presence in these virtual worlds is on the rise. Faculty from Trinity University in San Antonio, University of Texas at Austin, San Francisco State University, Rochester Institute of Technology,

Southern New Hampshire University, and Vassar College are using Second Life in their courses (Graetz 2006; Terdiman 2004). Even Harvard Law School has a presence in Second Life. In the fall 2006 semester, Harvard law professor Charles Nesson teamed up with his daughter, an instructor at the Harvard Extension School, to teach "CyberOne: Law in the Court of Public Opinion." Students have the option of taking the course in Harvard's real-life Ames Courtroom or in a virtual replica of the courtroom that resides in Second Life (Foster 2006).

As our faculty begin to explore the possibilities and pedagogical potential of virtual worlds, it will be important that their libraries and librarians accompany them, lest we are replaced by new knowledge partners in the virtual world.

Collection Development

Although many academic libraries have expanded their collection development scope to include audio and video media, not many are adding gaming software to their collections. As with DVD and audio e-books, public libraries in general have been quicker than academic libraries to build collections of computer gaming software. Some academic libraries do collect small amounts of "leisure" materials that provide more in the way of entertainment and relaxation than educational stimulation, such as motion picture DVDs and popular romance and science fiction novels. Gaming software could fit quite nicely into these diversionary collections. Squire and Steinkuehler (2005, 41) recommend the following games as a possible beginning for a library collection: Civilization III, Sim City, Age of Empires, Rome: Total War, Age of Mythology, The Sims, Roller Coaster Tycoon, Pikmin, Animal Crossing, Sid Meier's Pirates!, Rise of Nations, Ico, and Deus Ex. Examples of growing gaming collections can be seen at the libraries of the University of Illinois at Urbana-Champaign and Stanford University.[10]

If gaming software were available for loan from the library, there is little doubt that the collection would be heavily used. The number of students who are bringing gaming consoles such as PlayStations and Xboxes to college with them is on the rise. Gaming consoles are becoming as common in dorm rooms as televisions and DVD players. As evidence, see the many university residential network websites that detail how to configure game consoles onto the university network.[11]

Of course, using collection development money to purchase game software means that those funds are being diverted from the purchase of other more traditional academic library materials. If the interest in building a gaming software collection is high enough among Net Generation students, undergraduate and graduate student organizations may wish to contribute from their funds to support such a collection.

Another way an academic library can support gaming through collection development is suggested by Squire and Steinkuehler (2005). Playing games can spawn new interests, which in turn cause gamers to seek reading materials in order to learn more about the topic. For example, players of American Civil War: Gettysburg may want reading materials about the war and period that can provide context to the events of the game. By searching the names of popular games in MySpace and Facebook, you can get a sense of which games are currently popular with your students.

As gaming becomes a more mainstream pastime and an important element in popular culture, academic libraries should begin to develop collections of books and journals about gaming. To find some recent monographs, search OCLC's Worldcat using subject headings such as "Internet games—Social aspects" and "Computer games—Psychological aspects." Gallaway (2005, 14) recommends carrying the following journal titles: *Computer Gaming World, Dragon, Electronic Gaming Monthly, Game Informer, GamePro, Nintendo Power, Official Xbox, PC Gamer, Play,* and *Tips and Tricks.* With the emergence of gaming curricula and degree programs on campuses, such as Rochester Institute of Technology's master's degree in game design and development, library materials will be required to support this new scholarly pursuit.

Public Services

An academic library's response to online gaming should extend beyond collection development. Just as gaming can provide pedagogical benefits to the academic classroom, so too can it increase the learning potential of library instruction. At the University of Waterloo Library, Christy Branston, liaison librarian for government information and economics, has created a series of team-based online games as the delivery mechanism for government information instruction.[12]

Branston's idea could, and should, be extended into other areas of library instructional content. Imagine tutorials on how to use LexisNexis or ISI's Web of Science in the form of online games. These individual tutorials could then be pulled together to create an overarching game framework, through which students begin to develop a mastery of library research. Just as players can build up their skill levels in EverQuest, so too could students build virtual status in this virtual library world. When a student needs assistance and is not comfortable approaching a librarian, perhaps she will instead seek a peer with higher skill levels within the game.

MMORPGs also suggest some alternatives to the traditional library reference desk model. For example, when a player requires assistance he can "yell," which broadcasts to those avatars nearby that help is needed. A player who has the time, inclination, and skills to help will often volunteer to do so. This help model differs from a library reference desk in at least two key points. One is that the burden does not fall to the person in need to travel to receive assistance, such as to the reference desk. Instead, the individual stays put and the helpers come to him.

College students rarely leave their dorm room without their cell phones in hand. Although cognizant of this fact, most academic libraries do not do enough to take advantage of this fact. Few libraries post the phone numbers of the reference desk prominently and numerously inside the library itself, because the assumption is that the students should come to the desk in person. This is, however, rarely a practical alternative for a student, who would first need to pack up her textbooks and laptop computer, else risk their theft while she is away from her study location. Or, if the student is using a public computer terminal and there is a long line of students waiting to use it, she will likely lose her computer or annoy her fellow students for not surrendering the computer when she is not physically at it.

The MMORPG "yell" system suggests that the reference desk service model needs to be reversed. It should be the reference librarians who physically come to the student when help is needed. It makes more sense to push the burden onto the helper, not the person in need of help, particularly if the communications devices students always carry with them could be used to make this system possible.

The second difference between a reference desk and the MMORPG help paradigm is that the request for help goes out to everyone, not just to appointed helpers such as reference librarians. A student studying in the library may need help with his economics problem set and would likely receive far better assistance from a classmate or an economics major than from the reference librarian. Again, the burden should not fall to the person in need to determine to whom he should turn for assistance. Rather, it should be those capable of assistance who make that determination. If we could create the real-life counterpart to the virtual yell for help, then the academic library could become the place students go for academic assistance, regardless of whether it fits within the narrower sense of library assistance. The librarians, of course, would be active participants in this new help system, but not the only important participants. This system would build a strong sense of campus community, and essentially the library would be fostering the peer-to-peer support environment that most academic campuses struggle so hard to create.

The model of online games also suggests ways to alleviate the anxiety associated with libraries. The phenomenon of library anxiety is both well documented and surprisingly widespread (Onwuegbuzie, Jiao, and Bostick 2004). As Branston suggests, MMORPGs and other online games may reveal ways we can alleviate some of the library anxiety, or at least make it more constructive:

> The unknown and the discovery factor in learning and playing a game are a big part of the appeal. Being thrown into a new environment and learning to survive is half the fun. Imagine if our students viewed learning how to use the library in the same light as they do learning how to navigate around a new world in a video game. They need not fear it—the discovery should be fun. If we can borrow techniques from video games, libraries might be able to push past their intimidating reputations. (2006, 26)

One way to do this is for librarians to strive to be present themselves as "a strategy guide, rather than an authority" (Gallaway 2005, 16). Success in a MMORPG comes from designing and implementing successful strategies, because there is rarely a single, correct solution. Gamers regularly seek advice about new strategies from players with higher skill levels. Similarly, successful library research comes not from knowing the single, correct way to conduct research but instead by building a tool kit of successful strategies that can be applied in different types of situations. If librarians could present themselves as strategy guides, they might be able to adapt a role that is familiar to the many Net Gen students who are casual or avid game players while avoiding the anxiety-causing role of librarian as authority.

Physical Facilities

When libraries began including video and audio media in their collections, they had to make some changes to the physical facilities as well. New furniture and equipment were required to create viewing booths and listening stations that allowed groups of students to watch or listen to multimedia materials comfortably. Public terminals had to be configured with improved video and sound cards, speakers were added, and the audio jacks had to be made easily accessible.

We should expect that these same sorts of changes will be needed as academic libraries adjust to the new gaming medium. If your library is going to support online games actively, students must be able to load and download gaming software on the public computers. How else could a student who does not own a computer attend a class discussion group in Second Life or complete his physics homework, which is to play a round of Roller Coaster Tycoon? Highly graphic online games require fast Internet connections and computers with fast processors. Moreover, they are best viewed on a computer screen with a generous size and high resolution.

Some games require joysticks and other special input devices. Would this be any different than lending headphones to students who want to listen to a CD? If you would prefer that students bring their own laptops to the libraries, remember that highly graphic computer games quickly exhaust a laptop battery, so the demand for power outlets in the library will only increase. Moreover, the bandwidth of most wireless systems is currently insufficient to relay the real-time activities of a MMORPG, so students will need jacks to connect their laptops to the Internet physically.

There are even emerging lines of furniture designed specifically for gamers. Gaming rockers sit low on the floor and usually have built-in speakers that can connect with a computer or gaming console's audio outputs. Some are made like beanbags and sell for less than $30; others cost hundreds of dollars and are as sophisticated as today's office computer chair. An academic library could consider purchasing these types of gaming furniture as a way to both accommodate the playing of games and send a visual message that the library embraces the gaming culture.

In the same vein, Sutton and Womack (2006), Squire and Steinkuehler (2005), and Branston (2006) all suggest that libraries should host gaming nights. Such events may bring students into the library who otherwise feel they had no reason to be there. They may also cause students to rethink their misconception of an academic library as just the place where the old books are stored (De Rosa et al. 2005).

Library's Online Presence

An academic library's website can borrow many useful ideas from online games. Often library buildings, after years of building add-ons, are labyrinths of book stacks. The confusion students encounter in the stacks is a significant deterrent to using a library's collection. One way to alleviate this problem is to create a navigable, virtual replica of the library. This would make for a great project for an upper-level computer programming class. Once built, the virtual replica of the library could be used as a tool for finding books: click on the call number of an item in the catalog, and the item's location is marked in the virtual library, with visual and written directions from the location of the computer terminal the student is using. The virtual library could also be the locale for a entertaining computer game (another project for a computer programming class), where the by-product of playing the game is familiarity with the library's physical building.

Academic libraries cannot afford to ignore the growing interest in online gaming. As this chapter suggests, playing computer games is not merely a diversionary activity. Inside well-designed games rests great learning potential. As more educational games are developed and the acceptance of computer games as a teaching tool increases, academic libraries will feel increased pressure to find ways to support the medium. Why not get a head start right now?

NOTES

1. For examples, see http://zone.msn.com/en/root/default.htm, http://www.holdempoker.com, or http://www.gamezone.com/ongaming/p12660.htm.
2. See http://swvault.ign.com/View.php?view=Movies.List&category_select_id=3. I must credit Paula Le Dieu, former director of iCommons, for first using the cantina crawls as an example of the fostering of collaborative creativity in virtual games.
3. Quoted from http://mypage.iu.edu/~castro/home.html.
4. Quoted from http://www.lineage.com/guide/char_pledges.html.
5. Quoted from http://www.pps.org/info/placemakingtools/placemakers/roldenburg/.
6. Quoted from http://muve.gse.harvard.edu/rivercityproject/index.html.
7. Quoted from http://swi.indiana.edu.
8. See http://www.udel.edu/mserc/mfme/coaster.html.
9. See http://www.usiouxfalls.edu/professionalstudies/dcp/syllabi/59/bus392.pdf.
10. See http://www.library.uiuc.edu/gaming/, and http://library.stanford.edu/depts/hasrg/histsci/atari_list.htm.
11. For examples, see http://resnet.ramapo.edu/config_game.php, http://www.housing.wisc.edu/resnet/gameConsoles.php, and http://its.syr.edu/rescom/gameconsoles.cfm.
12. See http://www.lib.uwaterloo.ca/staff/isr/gp2/game.html.

CHAPTER FOUR

Web 2.0

ONLINE GAMES ARE NOT THE ONLY ROUTE TO AN engaging experience on the Net. The rest of the Web is rapidly catching up.

The Web has never been a purely static experience, but it has not been all that interactive either. With the vast majority of web pages, when a user arrives at the page of HTML code, displayed through an Internet browser, there is usually little more than text to be read and images to be viewed. Movement through the website is accomplished through user-initiated mouse clicks, to which the web server responds with a repeatable, usually predictable, response. The delivery of content is predominantly a one-way conversation, with the website, as proxy for its author, the speaker and the web surfer the listener. A productive experience with the Web requires the user to be able to locate and pull the appropriate web pages out of the vast sea of possible websites. This is the familiar world of Web 1.0 to which the majority of us have grown accustomed.

The concept of Web 2.0 promises to be very different. Tim O'Reilly, founder and CEO of O'Reilly Media, is credited with coining the term "Web 2.0" in 2004. Although there is certainly no consensus about what Web 2.0 fully entails, there are some shared principles, which were presented by O'Reilly in 2005 and are captured in figure 4-1. The first is the concept of "the Web as platform." In the Web 1.0 world, a website with its static text and images is the deliverable. In the 2.0 world, however, the Web is just the platform or foundation, which supports the delivery of myriad dynamic services.

O'Reilly (2005) uses Google to demonstrate the concept of the Web as platform:

> Google's service is not a server—though it is delivered by a massive collection of internet servers—nor a browser—though it is experienced by the user

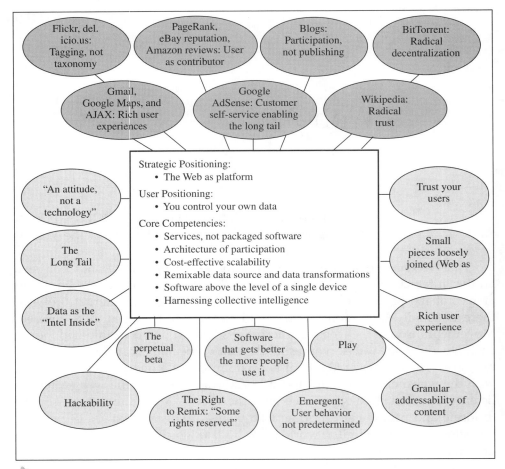

FIGURE 4-1
Web 2.0 meme map. Originally published in Tim O'Reilly's "What Is Web 2.0"
(http://tim.oreilly.com/news/2005/09/30what-is-web-20.html)

within the browser. Nor does its flagship search service even host the content
it enables users to find. . . . Google happens in the space between browser
and search engine and destination content server, as an enabler or middleman
between the user and his or her online experience.

The Web has become a computing platform that can deliver a dizzying array of
services through little more than a web browser, thereby eliminating the need
for the end user to install special software on her own personal computer. As

Google makes incremental changes to its product, we never have to download or install new releases. Rather, the web platform hosts these product changes on our behalf.

The second principle of Web 2.0 is the "harnessing of collective intelligence." In the 1.0 world, when a user arrives and engages a website, that interaction has little consequence for the website, except to add another hit to the usage statistics. With Web 2.0 products, it is the user's engagement with the website that literally drives it. Amazon.com is an excellent example of this. Each time you visit Amazon.com, you leave behind a virtual pile of useful data. The search terms you use, the sequence of books you examine, the reviews you read and write, and ultimately the books you buy are collected and combined with similar data from other users to form an enormous body of information about user behavior. Buried within are discernable patterns, which, once recognized, can be leveraged and turned into new and improved features. For example, Amazon.com is using this immense collection of past usage data to create the features "Customers who bought this item also bought . . ." and "What do customers ultimately buy after viewing items like this?" which are marvelous recommender systems that no one person alone could create.

Digg (digg.com) is another example of a website harnessing the collective intelligence of its users. Digg users submit links to news stories they have found interesting. As explained on the website, "After you submit content, other digg users read your submission and digg [vote for] what they like best. If your story rocks and receives enough diggs, it is promoted to the front page for the millions of digg visitors to see." The result is a news outlet where the community of users, not an elite group of individuals, act as the editors.

The third Web 2.0 principle is the primacy of data and the databases that house it. At the core of Google's service is an immense database of metadata for billions of web pages. A database of available books is at the core of Amazon.com; MapQuest (www.mapquest.com) rests on a database of maps. The successful firms of Web 2.0 are those that not only have the best data but also know how to harness it well. For example, although the book data Amazon.com controls is quite similar to that within a library catalog and Bowker's *Books in Print,* the presentation, channeling, and harnessing of this data are strikingly different. Few would argue with the assessment that Amazon.com does a far better job than a library catalog of realizing the full potential of that data.

The "end of the software release cycle" is O'Reilly's fourth principle. Successful Web 2.0 companies do not have rigid, predetermined software releases. Instead, the software is tweaked and improved on an ongoing, sometimes daily basis, dependent upon a continuous flow of user feedback.

This feedback is obtained by direct means, such as through a customer comment system, but also indirectly via the "real time monitoring of user behavior to see just which new features are used, and how they are used" (O'Reilly 2005). This continuous cycle of improvement actually places website users in the role of "codevelopers," whether they are conscious of this or not. Moreover, it means that a Web 2.0 product is in "perpetual beta" because there is never an official, finished product.

O'Reilly's fifth principle is the reliance on lightweight programming models. A website undergoing continual change requires simplicity. Instead of tightly intertwining the various components of a website, Web 2.0 products strive for loosely coupled, often modular systems that allow pieces to be swapped in and out easily. The sixth principle pushes this flexibility of options to the end user. The Web is no longer limited to personal computers but can embrace a whole suite of devices. For example, the digital music distribution company iTunes (www.apple.com/itunes/) and TiVo (www.tivo.com), a personal digital recorder of television, "are not web applications per se, but they leverage the power of the web platform, making it a seamless, almost invisible part of their infrastructure" (O'Reilly 2005).

When these principles are combined and actualized, the Web becomes a more interactive, dynamic experience for all users. There is, in essence, a continuous dialogue between the users and the web pages they encounter, and the result is an increasingly personalized, customized experience. This rich user experience need not, however, stop at the outer edges of an academic library's website. Rather, the concept of Library 2.0 has been recently posited by several writers (see, e.g., Casey and Savastinuk 2006; Chad and Miller 2005; Miller 2005, 2006a, 2006b).

> Library 2.0 is a concept of a very different library service, geared towards the needs and expectations of today's library users. In this vision, the library makes information available wherever and whenever the user requires it, and seeks to ensure that barriers to use and reuse are removed. (Miller 2006b, 2)

In other words, the same concepts and technologies that are creating the Web 2.0 experience should also be used to build the Library 2.0 experience.

Actualizing Web 2.0 is a growing set of simple yet powerful tools that are turning the Web into an interactive, context-rich, and highly personalized experience. This list of tools is continually expanding, and consequently any attempt to mention them all is rather futile. There are, however, several tools that have become the 2006 poster children for Web 2.0. This small subset is our focus for the remainder of this chapter and the next.

RSS

RSS, an acronym for Really Simple Syndication or Rich Site Summary, denotes a class of web feeds, specified in XML (Extensible Markup Language). In layperson's terms, RSS is a way to syndicate the content of a website. From a user's perspective, this means that you do not have to visit a website continually to see if there is new information. Instead, you subscribe to the RSS feed, and every time the website changes an RSS feed is sent, alerting you to the change.

RSS feeds are easier to explain with an example. Suppose you are an avid reader of the *New York Times* online. Throughout the day, the *Times* website is regularly updated with breaking stories, and you find yourself constantly returning to www.nytimes.com to see what has been added since the last time you visited the site. RSS feeds provide an alternative to this time-consuming process. Instead of visiting the *Times* website again and again, you could subscribe to the *Times* RSS feeds. Whenever something is added, the headline, a short summary, and a link back to the full article are sent to your RSS reader (explained below). Although the *Times* has an all-encompassing RSS feed, it has also divided up its content into smaller, more refined feeds. Consequently, if your interest is only in "International News," "College Basketball," or "Movie Reviews," you can subscribe to a feed limited to just that topic.

An RSS reader is the receiver and aggregator of all the RSS feeds you are receiving. The RSS reader can come in many different forms. Some readers work by sending you the RSS feed through your e-mail. As an example, "Blog Alert" is a free system that sends you daily e-mail notifications of new RSS feeds.[1] No special software is needed. Just enter the URL of the RSS feed and your e-mail address into the web form, and the e-mail alerts start arriving daily.

If you would prefer not to clog your e-mail in-box, there are many RSS reader applications available for download onto your computer. Awasu (www.awasu.com), for example, is a free RSS reader that runs on Window computers. Through a rich graphic interface, Awasu keeps track of all your subscribed RSS feeds and alerts you when something new arrives. As your list of RSS subscriptions grows, you can arrange the feeds into categories, or channels. The software keeps track of what you have already read so that you are not looking at the same content repeatedly.

If, however, you use many different computers throughout the day, you can avoid loading an RSS reader application onto all of them and eliminate the inevitable synchronization problems (e.g., you read a feed on your office computer, but your home computer still has it marked as new and unread) by using a web-based reader such as Bloglines (www.bloglines.com; see fig. 4-2). Any time you have access to the Web, you can log into your Bloglines account and get your latest RSS feeds. Registration and setup are simple and currently free.

In 2005 the Pew Internet and American Life Project found that 5% of Internet users in the United States use RSS readers "to get the news and other information delivered from blogs and content-rich Web sites as it is posted online" (Rainie 2005, 1). Although 5% may not seem significant, it becomes a much more impressive number when translated into 6 million Americans. RSS feeds can be used to stay current on content from a wide variety of information sources including formal news outlets (e.g., *New York Times* and CNN.com), publishers (e.g., *Nature* and the U.S. Government Printing Office), alerting services (e.g., National Hurricane Center), and vendors (e.g., Target and iTunes Store). The bottom line is that RSS feeds are a cost-effective and time-effective way for anyone to stay current in this fast-paced, digital world.

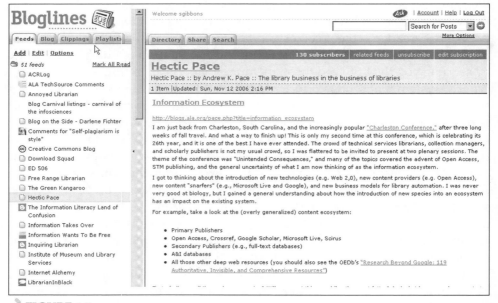

FIGURE 4-2
Author's RSS feeds in the Bloglines RSS reader, displaying an entry from Andrew K. Pace's blog *Hectic Pace*

Blogs

In addition to the list above, one could also subscribe to the RSS feeds of interesting blogs. The term "blog" is actually a shortened version of the word "weblog." Wikipedia describes a blog as "a type of website where entries are made (such as in a journal or diary), and displayed in reverse chronological order."[2] Blogs are simply online journals in which writers can easily jot down their thoughts or comments, accompanied by any related links. It has always been possible for a plain HTML website to function as an online diary, but the popularity of blogs really began to flourish in the late 1990s with the availability of free and cheap blogging platforms such as Xanga (www.xanga.com), LiveJournal (www.livejournal.com), and Blogger (www.blogger.com).

An individual's blog is a personal communications venue through which to share thoughts, comments, beliefs, rants, and raves with the world. A 2006 national survey by the Pew Internet and American Life Project found that 8% of Internet users in the United States (about 12 million adults) keep a blog. There are, however, significantly more blog readers, with an active audience of approximately 57 million American adults (Lenhart and Fox 2006, i). Over the past three years, the number of blogs has doubled every six months, with close to 175,000 new ones created each day. The total number of blogs exceeded 50 million in July 2006 (Lanchester 2006).

Blogger demographics are interesting. Only 54% are under the age of 30, with an even split between male and female. Half of all bloggers live in the suburbs, and a third live in urban areas. Surprisingly, African Americans and English-speaking Hispanics have a greater representation in the blogger population than in the general Internet population (Lenhart and Fox 2006, ii).

For the vast majority of bloggers (84%), blogging is just a hobby or casual pastime. Although some of the highest-profile blogs focus on politics, such as *Daily Kos* (www.dailykos.com) and *Crooks and Liars* (www.crooksandliars.com), the most popular blogging topic (37%) is actually focused on one's life and experiences. Although blogging is by its nature a public activity, the Pew study found that "most bloggers view it as a personal pursuit," and yet 87% of bloggers allow comments on their blogs, suggesting an awareness of visitors (Lenhart and Fox 2006, ii, iv).

As with RSS readers, blogs can be hosted locally or remotely. Locally installed blogging software such as Movable Type (www.movabletype.org) is more feature rich and able to support significant customizations and branding. As Stephens (2006, 27) notes, however, the software can be difficult to install and requires some level of technical and programming support. The remotely hosted blogging systems, including Blogger and WordPress (wordpress.org), are accessible from any computer with an Internet connection and require no technical expertise or support. Customization is, however, limited, and the blogs reside on the host's branded site as just one of several thousand hosted by the service.

The mechanics for creating a blog entry are quite simple. Through a straightforward, web-based form, the author enters text and adds any relevant links and images. When the entry is complete, the author submits the entry and it then automatically appears at the top of the blog, date and time stamped. The blog owner/author can elect to make the blog public to the world or available to just a subset of people and can decide whether to allow others to comment on the blog entries. (See fig. 4-3.)

Accompanying the explosion in the number of blogs is the emergence of blog-specific search engines that crawl the "blogosphere." Popular examples of these include Technorati (www.technorati.com), Feedster (www.feedster.com), and IceRocket (www.icerocket.com).

Wikis

Blogs essentially follow a diary metaphor, with the entries in reverse chronological order and "penned" by a single, primary author. Wikis, on the other

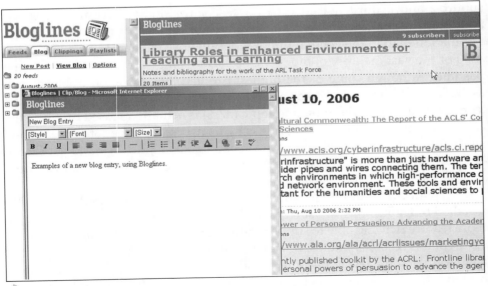

FIGURE 4-3
Screen shot demonstrating how to create a blog entry in Bloglines

hand, are subject-driven information sites that deliberately have a shared and distributed authorship (Ferris and Wilder 2006). *Wiki* is the Hawaiian word for "quick," which characterizes the speed with which a person can use a wiki. A wiki, as described by the world's most popular instantiation of it, Wikipedia, "is a type of website that allows the visitors themselves to easily add, remove and otherwise edit and change some available content, sometimes without the need for registration."[3]

The basic component of a wiki is a web page with some informational content. Without the use of any special locally hosted software, a person can click on a page's "edit" button, make changes to the content, and then save those changes. All of the older versions of the page are saved in a history log, whereby errors or malicious acts can be corrected by simply reverting to an older version of the page.

Because wikis can allow literally anyone to add or edit their content, one might presume that the outcome would be of poor quality or chaotic form. In reality, it is the highly collaborative nature of wikis that ensure both quality and order. Wikis harness the power of collective knowledge, because presumably no single person could possibly create all the content. Rather, anyone with expertise, knowledge, interest, or enthusiasm can contribute to the effort. In addition, the numerous sets of eyes that work with the content ensure a high level of quality: "It is the community of users acting as quality control that keeps content in-line and on-topic" (Guenther 2005, 53).

As with RSS readers and blogs, there are many wiki software options available, with a range in complexity. At the easier end of the scale are the open-source Tipiwiki (tipiwiki.sourceforge.net) and JotSpot (www.jot.com), which was acquired by Google in 2006. The more complex and fuller-featured wikis include Tikiwiki (tikiwiki.org) and the German system MoinMoin (moinmoin .wikiwikiweb.de). Tonkin (2005) and Stephens (2006) provide useful overviews of the features and functionalities of available wikis.

Wikis are used as the foundation of all sorts of projects. For example, the wiki Memory Alpha is a large and popular encyclopedic reference for all things related to Star Trek.[4] There are wikis focused on political campaigns, comic books, travel, and cooking. Wikis can be found in many different languages as well, including French, Polish, Russian, Esperanto, Kurdish, and Bengali.[5]

By far the best-known wiki is Wikipedia (en.wikipedia.org), an immense, collaboratively authored encyclopedia. Founded in January 2001 by Larry Sanger and Jimmy Wales, Wikipedia began as "an effort to create and distribute a multi-lingual free encyclopedia of the highest possible quality to every single person on the planet in their own language."[6] Literally anyone can contribute to Wikipedia by adding new entries or editing the entries that already exist, and the result thus far has been quite astonishing.

In mid-October 2006, Wikipedia had close to 2.5 million registered contributors. English-language entries alone numbered more than 1.43 million, and when combined with articles in the more than two hundred non-English languages the number jumps to 4.6 million. Wikipedia's rate of growth is astounding. In July 2006 alone it grew by 30 million words, leading to the conclusion that even "a fast reader could never catch up with Wikipedia's content."[7]

The entries in Wikipedia strive to be unbiased, as explained in Wikipedia's policy of NPOV, or "neutral point of view."[8] Entries should report only facts, not opinions or rumors. Moreover, they should strive to provide a balanced presentation of all possible viewpoints. Although some argue that no act of writing can be completely devoid of the author's biases, the NPOV policy is taken quite seriously.

Wikipedia is certainly not without controversy, particularly with regard to the quality of its content. The Nature Publishing Group decided to test the general presumption that Wikipedia, because it is the collaborative creation of millions of volunteers, is inferior to a formal encyclopedia of the caliber of *Encyclopaedia Britannica.* The result of this Wikipedia/*Britannica* comparison "revealed numerous errors in both encyclopaedias, but among 42 entries tested, the difference in accuracy was not particularly great: the average science entry in Wikipedia contained around four inaccuracies; Britannica, about three." Although accuracy did not greatly differ between the two, the *Nature* reviews did note that the *Britannica* articles were generally more readable, "commenting that the Wikipedia articles they reviewed [were] poorly structured and confusing" (Giles 2005). Consequently, when Internet users are seeking accurate, free information, Wikipedia appears to be a respectable source, although it may lack the clarity and readability of *Britannica.* The growing respectability of Wikipedia combined with its astonishing use and growth led Poe (2006) to speculate that "Wikipedia has the potential to be the greatest effort in collaborative knowledge gathering the world has ever known, and it may well be the greatest effort in voluntary collaboration of any kind."

RSS, Blogs, and Wikis in Academic Libraries

Academic libraries can harness the power of RSS feeds, blogs, and wikis in numerous ways. For example, libraries can use RSS feeds to push information out to their patrons. Many libraries post news and events items on their home page, which can be turned into RSS feeds. You can see examples of this on the library websites of the University of Michigan (www.lib.umich.edu), Princeton University (libweb.princeton.edu), and Northwestern University (www.library.northwestern.edu/rssinfo.html).

New book lists can also be distributed via RSS feeds, as is done at the libraries of the University of Alabama, Case Western Reserve University, and University of Nevada, Reno.[9] It is also possible to add RSS feeds to the library catalog whereby students can sign up for an alert whenever the results of a particular search have changed. For example, the Hennepin County Library (www.hclib.org) has programmed RSS feeds into its catalog:

> Run any keyword search in the HCL catalog, and at the top of the search results, you'll find an RSS button that lets you *subscribe to* or *syndicate* that search. . . . [T]he next time a member of the HCL staff adds a record with that phrase in it, you'll be notified. (Stephens 2006, 39)

A library can also add RSS feeds to its subject guides and course pages. Many of the subject guides developed by the College of New Jersey Library include an RSS feed sidebar of recent acquisitions in the respective subject area. The University of Pennsylvania has created the Library RSS Feed Generator, with which the UPenn community can generate RSS feeds for any broad subject area of interest. Ball State Library uses the technology as a means to push out communications from library liaisons.[10]

The integrated library system vendor Talis is investigating the use of RSS in libraries through its Project Bluebird. Talis proposes a list of library RSS applications that include

- lists of new books
- warnings that an item will become overdue in the next x days
- new reading lists
- advice that a requested item is now ready for pick up
- end-of-term reminders
- alerts that potential charges have reached a given amount
- virtual book groups' shared reviews
- distributions of sound samples for newly available music CDs
- library news such as changes to opening hours[11]

Libraries can also aggregate the RSS feeds of others and repackage them in useful ways. The University of Wisconsin–Madison has brought together the RSS feeds of some of its e-journals onto a single page that a student or faculty member can browse and then subscribe to where interested.[12] Many journals and databases do not, however, provide RSS feeds. Fortunately, David Walker of California State University has solved this problem with his RSS Creator system: "RSS Creator is a system that allows us to create RSS feeds for any journal or newspaper indexed and abstracted in our current subscription databases."[13] By using the data stored within his SFX Knowledge base, Walker's system can create an RSS feed for any journal or newspaper that is currently searchable via the library's federated search tool, Metalib.

Another way to capitalize on the power of RSS is by syndicating the library's content and news in order to increase the places where users can encounter it. If a library provides RSS feeds, they can be repackaged by others into more comprehensive services. At the University of Utah, the library's RSS feeds have been combined with the other news feeds on campus into a comprehensive university news and events service.[14] RSS feeds from the Harvey Cushing/John Hay Whitney Medical Library at Yale University are pulled into YaleInfo, the university's portal.

Another example of syndication can be seen at the College of New Jersey. There the library's feeds are available through the college's course management system, where they are prominently displayed. Through these feeds, the library is able to push notices about recent book acquisitions that are directly relevant to the curriculum of the course (Corrado, Moulaison, and Thul 2006). As a result, not only is the information delivered into a digital tool that the students use regularly, but the library is able to place its resources directly into a context that is highly relevant to the students—their courses.

RSS feeds are also a valuable tool to help library staff stay current. There is an ever-growing corpus of library-related blogs that highlight news, events, innovations, and best practices important to librarianship. Technorati lists close to two hundred blogs tagged with the term "library," including Jenny Levine's *The Shifted Librarian, Lorcan Dempsey's weblog,* Brian Mathews's *Ubiquitous Librarian,* and Andrew Pace's *Hectic Pace.*[15] Subscribing to the RSS feeds of these blogs is an excellent way for librarians to keep on top of the latest library trends.

RSS feeds and blogs can be used to keep a finger on the pulse of one's local campus as well. Mathews (2006b) recommends that librarians regularly read the blogs of students on campus, which are often identifiable by their academic affiliations. One easy way to find these local blogs is to search on the name of your institution or library in one of the blog search engines, such as Technorati. While monitoring the local blogs at Georgia Tech University, Mathews found opportunities to answer reference-like questions, market library services and library workshops, and keep on top of problems and criticisms of the library. "Instead of forcing patrons to interact with us, we can enter their domain and seek new ways of providing assistance. By monitoring blogs, librarians can step beyond their traditional role and serve as teachers, mentors, and counselors" (2006b, 2).

Stephens (2006) suggests many types of blogs a library could consider adding to its web presence, including these:

- library news blogs, such as those at Binghamton University and Dartmouth College library[16]
- materials/resources blogs that highlight different parts of the library's collection, like UNC–Chapel Hill's North Carolina Miscellany[17]
- project-specific blogs, such as the Tufts University renovation blog[18]
- user-specific blogs that focus on patron subsections, for example, Library News for Distance Learners at Middle Tennessee State University[19]

Blogs can be added to subject and class resources guides, but they can also serve as the guide itself. Librarians can build resource guides with blogs, thus eliminating the need for them to learn how to edit website pages, which can be a technology barrier.

A more sophisticated use of blogs can be seen at Plymouth State University. Here the concept of a WPopac was developed, which is essentially an OPAC (online public access catalog) "inside the framework of WordPress, the hugely popular blog management application."[20] It combines the data from the traditional library catalog with the interactive features of a blog, including commenting and tagging. Although still just a proof-of-concept, the project gives a glimpse of the impact blogs could have on the way academic libraries deliver content and, more important, solicit participation from their students and faculty.

Blogs are a way to invite comment from your user community, literally, through the blog's comment feature. Still, a blog has a primary author, and commenters play a secondary role. If you want a true, collaborative partnership with your academic community, then consider a wiki. As students research a topic for a course, they could collaborate with the subject librarian on a wiki of relevant library resources. A wiki could also be used to gather student comments and feedback about library services, renovation plans, or website redesign. For example, a library's subject and course resource guides could be built with a wiki, and together the librarian and users of the guide could work together to create and maintain it. The Ohio University Libraries have wikis for business information resources and film, theater, and literature.[21]

Library-hosted blogs need not, however, mandate librarian participation. It can be equally as important for academic libraries to provide blogging platforms for students but then take a backseat and let the students be the drivers. Lippincott suggests that "libraries should explore blogs as mechanisms for students to exchange information on valuable information resources they find for particular course assignments" (2005, 13.8). An excellent example is at the University of Minnesota Libraries, which provides a blog hosting service for the university community:

> [The University of Minnesota] Libraries believe passionately in intellectual and academic freedom, and our role as advocates for those freedoms. Blogs are an excellent tool whereby students, faculty and staff at the University can let their opinions be heard. Blogs offer a way to rapidly discuss opinions, issues, and ideas, and allow people from across the country, and campus, to connect with each other through these ideas.[22]

The service, branded UThink, is free and now hosts more than 3,600 blogs from the university community that cover a huge spectrum of categories including music, food, movies, travel, digital narrative, and books.

RSS feeds, blogs, and wikis are just a few of the tools that are transforming the Web 1.0 experience into Web 2.0. RSS feeds are a way to begin the process of pushing library content beyond the walls of the physical and virtual academic library. But doing this requires us librarians to relinquish some control over how this library information is presented. For example, RSS feeds about new materials purchased by the library may be useful to many within your academic community. But once that information is openly distributed and shared, it can invite students and faculty to question the library's purchases. Or, in another case, you may disagree with the placement of the library's RSS feeds in the university's portal; perhaps it has been clustered with parking and other "auxiliary services," when you believe it should be a part of the academic cluster. Pushing library content beyond a library's walls means that your community can interact with it at point of need (e.g., in a course management system) or in a more convenient and efficient manner (e.g., in an RSS reader). But it also means that you must relinquish control over how that information is used and where.

Currently there are few examples of academic library applications of wikis, because they require a high degree of trust—trust that your users, particularly undergraduate students, will take the building of a resource guide as seriously as you do. On the one hand, wikis are attractive because they are both transparent and inclusive. They provide an open forum where anyone can contribute and thereby end the comment we all hate to hear: "How come I didn't know about that?" On the other hand, some people are wary about engaging an academic community, particularly students, in such an open, uncensored dialogue. Well, if Wikipedia can trust the entire world with its endeavor to create an online encyclopedia, why shouldn't we be able to do the same with our students?

Starting a blog or wiki can be threatening because it forces librarians out of the role of expert and into the more vulnerable role of guide and collaborator. But guides and collaborators, not experts, are what Net Generation students seem to be seeking, as a consequence of their team-focused upbringing. As Harder points out, "We've moved from a time when the web was mostly a 'read-only' technology, to an era where the many can now 'read-write-and-participate'" (2006, 54). Don't we want our library patrons to feel the same about our library websites? Imagine the sense of ownership and community that would foster.

NOTES

1. Find it at http://www.shootthebreeze.net/blogalert/index.php.
2. Quoted from http://en.wikipedia.org/wiki/Blogs.
3. Quoted from http://en.wikipedia.org/wiki/Wiki.
4. See http://memory-alpha.org/en/wiki/Main_Page/.
5. Regularly updated lists of wikis can be found at http://meta.wikimedia.org.
6. Quoted from http://en.wikipedia.org/wiki/Wikipedia.
7. Quoted from http://en.wikipedia.org/wiki/Wikipedia:Statistics.
8. Quoted from http://en.wikipedia.org/wiki/Wikipedia:Neutral_point_of_view.
9. For these examples, see http://library.ua.edu/rss/, http://library.case.edu/ksl/rss/, and http://www.library.unr.edu/ejournals/alphaRSS.aspx.
10. For these examples, see http://www.tcnj.edu/~library/research/subject_guides.html, http://www.library.upenn.edu/blos/feeds/index.html, and http://www.bsu.edu/library/rss/.
11. Adapted from http://www.talis.com/research/research/rss/RSSresearch.shtml.
12. Ebling Library RSS feeds at http://ebling.library.wisc.edu/bjd/journals/rss/index.cfm.
13. Quoted from http://public.csusm.edu/dwalker/rss_creator/2006/04/solution-for-rss-and-journals.html.
14. Available feeds at http://www.events.utah.edu/html/rssfeeds.html.
15. See these blogs at http://www.theshiftedlibrarian.com, http://orweblog.oclc.org, http://theubiquitouslibrarian.typepad.com/the_ubiquitous_librarian/, and http://blogs.ala.org/pace.php.
16. http://library.lib.binghamton.edu/mt/librarynews/ and http://library.dartmouth.edu/library/news/display.php.
17. http://www.lib.unc.edu/blogs/ncm/.
18. http://blogs.fletcher.tufts.edu/renovationblog/index.html.
19. http://www.distancelib.blogspot.com.
20. Quoted from http://maisonbisson.com/blog/post/11133/. See http://www.plymouth.edu/library/opac/.
21. See, for example, http://www.library.ohiou.edu/subjects/bizwiki/and http://www.library.ohiou.edu/subjects/litwiki/.
22. Quoted from http://blog.lib.umn.edu/about.html.

CHAPTER FIVE

Keeping Found
Things Found

WHILE BLOGS AND WIKIS ARE TRANSFORMING THE
Web from a soliloquy into a dialogue of countless voices,
another set of Web 2.0 tools, tagging and social bookmarking, is working to turn the generic Web into a much more personalized and
customized experience.

Tagging is the process of assigning keywords (tags) to an object that help
identify what the object is, why it is important, who owns it, and so on. This
should be a concept familiar to librarians, since tags are a type of metadata and
tagging is a kind of cataloging. What makes tagging different from traditional
cataloging can be found in who is tagging, why they are tagging, and to some
extent what they are tagging.

At the heart of tagging is a basic need—"keeping found things found"
(Bruce, Jones, and Dumais 2004). When a person creates a document or dis-
covers a useful one on the Web, she wants to be sure not to lose track of it. As
Gordon-Murnane explains, tagging "really has to do with retaining information
that you, I or anyone else has found and organizing it in a way so that people
can refind that information at a later date" (2006, 28). High personal benefits
can be derived from tagging because it addresses the problem we all have in
trying to keep track of everything in a digital world.

The perceived need for tagging emerges from two different computer-
related problems (Tonkin 2006). One is the limitations imposed by the file-
naming conventions of computers. The name of a computer file, such as a
Microsoft Word document, must follow the naming conventions dictated
by your computer's operating system, which limits the length of the name
and the types of characters that can be used. As a result, the retrieval of a
computer file can be quite difficult when the user fails to remember what she
called the file or cannot distinguish between files with similar names, such as
"biblio.doc," "bibliography.doc," and "referencelist.doc." Tagging takes much

of the burden away from computer file names to convey all of their relevant information within such a short string of characters; it is a way to break free of the limitations of computer file-naming conventions.

On the other hand, the enormity of the content on the Web, combined with its lax naming conventions and the absence of any standardized metadata schema, makes tagging attractive as well. In this case, tagging provides a way to tame the chaos and bring some personalized order to it. This problem resonates with many people and has given rise to personal information management (PIM) as both a field of study and a genre of new technologies, such as Chandler.[1] "It is interesting to note," writes Tonkin (2006), "that, as the trend towards more informal metadata continues in the file [naming] system, the trend towards formal metadata continues on the Web." Tagging offers a solution to both problems.

Tagging need not, however, be a private activity, particularly when you are tagging public websites, documents, and files on the Web. Other people may benefit from seeing your tags, and vice versa. It is exactly this potential for mutual benefit that has given rise to social bookmarking, which is the "practice of saving bookmarks to a public Web site and 'tagging' them with keywords" (EDUCAUSE Learning Initiative 2005). With social bookmarking, one's saved links, citations, and tags are made public and combined with those created by others. Once aggregated, the collection can be searched and browsed by everyone and serve as a discovery tool for related items of interest.

Gordon-Murnane (2006) cites three useful services provided by social bookmarking: (1) it helps the user organize and categorize collections of information, data, and content by allowing him to tag it in a personally meaningful way; (2) it allows the user to share his sources with others, which facilitates discovery by others; and (3) the collection of links is portable (web based) and is not tied to a particular computer or Internet browser; it is ubiquitous and your constant travel companion across the Web.

Moreover, social bookmarking can help you build social connections with other people with similar interests. As you use the bookmarks of others, you begin to notice the recurrence of certain user names. Social bookmarking services "act as excellent 'expert' discovery tools" (Etches-Johnson 2006, 57) by helping you find people who share similar research interests. Social bookmarking can draw you into a community of people with similar pursuits, many of whom you would not likely meet otherwise. Tonkin (2006) summarizes the benefits of tagging as "easy, enjoyable and quick to complete; it is an activity with low cognitive cost, which provides immediate self and social feedback."

How tagging and social bookmarking actually work can be easier to describe by using some screen shots and walking through the actual steps.

I have an account with a free social bookmarking service called del.icio.us. Within this account I can save the URLs of websites I find interesting and want to be able to find again later. When I save the URL, I also save some keyword tags with it so that I can recall why it is that I thought this site was useful.

In addition to my del.icio.us account, which resides on the Web at http://del.icio.us, I have downloaded and installed some del.icio.us buttons (bookmarklets) into my web browser, Firefox. When I find a website that I want to tag and save in my del.icio.us account, I just click on the del.icio.us "Tag" button. (See fig. 5-1.) Clicking this button causes a simple del.icio.us input

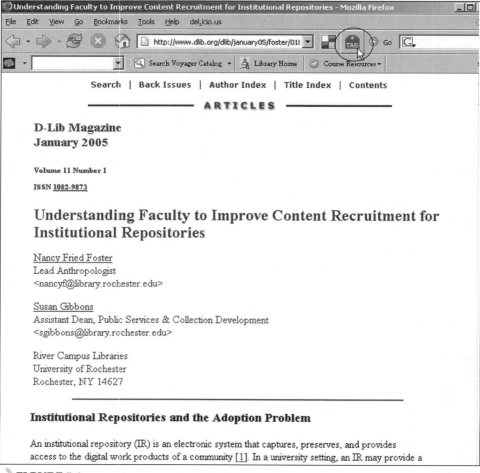

FIGURE 5-1
Firefox browser with the del.icio.us "Tag" button

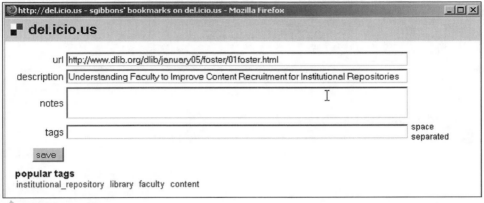

> **FIGURE 5-2**
> Input form in del.icio.us

form to open. The form has already captured the website's URL and title, but it gives me the option of adding personal notes and tags. I am also prompted with suggestions for tags to use, in this case "institutional_repository," "library," "faculty," and "content." (See fig. 5-2.)

Once I have saved this information, the bookmark shows up in my del.icio.us account. Each bookmark in my account becomes a vehicle for finding similar resources, such as other bookmarks that use the same tags, as well as other people who have saved this same resource. So, for example, following the tag "institutional_repository" leads to other resources that have also been tagged with "institutional_repository." (See figs. 5-3 and 5-4.)

On September 25, 2006, del.icio.us registered its one millionth user, making it the most popular social bookmarking service. What is quite astounding is how young the del.icio.us service actually is. Joshua Schachter created del.icio.us in order to manage his personal collection of web links better. He made the service public in September 2003, and then Yahoo! acquired it just two years later for an undisclosed amount that is rumored to be in the tens of millions of dollars. All the same, del.icio.us is just one of a growing number of free social bookmarking services. Furl (www.furl.net), which stands for File URLs, was created in 2003 by Michael Giles. (See fig. 5-5.) A distinguishing feature of Furl is that it not only saves the website link and tags you assign to it but also archives a personal copy of the web page. Users each have up to 5 gigabytes of storage in which to save cached web pages, so when a website is down, has

FIGURE 5-3
Author's del.icio.us bookmarks

changed significantly, or has been pulled from the Web, they still have access to the content. The free service was publicly launched in January 2004 and then acquired by LookSmart.

Two social bookmarking services have been designed specifically for academic audiences, CiteULike (www.citeulike.org) and Connotea (www .connotea.org). CiteULike was created and launched by Richard Cameron in

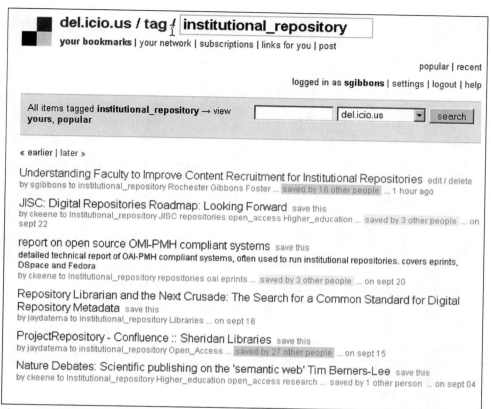

FIGURE 5-4
Bookmarks in del.icio.us with the "institutional_repository" tag

November 2004 and as of April 2007 continues to be run privately by Cameron (see fig. 5-6).

> CiteULike is a free service to help academics to share, store, and organize the academic papers they are reading. When you see a paper on the web that interests you, you can click one button and have it added to your personal library. CiteULike automatically extracts the citation details, so there's no need to type them in yourself. It all works from within your web browser. There's no need to install any special software.[2]

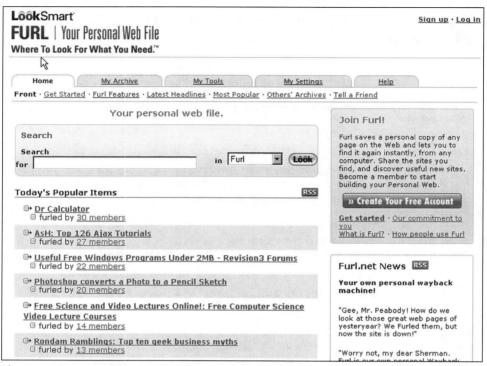

FIGURE 5-5
Home page of Furl

If CiteULike recognizes a website as one of the several dozen it is familiar with, such as PubMed Central, ACM Portal, Project Muse, or arXiv.org, it can automatically extract the citation data for you. If it does not recognize the site, then the citation data must be typed in manually. The system saves only the URL and not the document itself. Consequently, in the case of licensed content, the user must have a subscription to retrieve the actual document.

Connotea is a free social bookmarking system created by the Nature Publishing Group specifically for scientists and clinicians (see fig. 5-7). Connotea recognizes many scientific journals and websites and can automatically extract bibliographic data such as author, journal, and title from those web interfaces. Users have the option of making their bookmarks private or public. Citations can be easily imported and exported from Connotea, and a "bookmarklet" puts the "Add to Connotea" form just a click away. The source code for Connotea is freely available under the GNU General Public License from Sourceforge.[3]

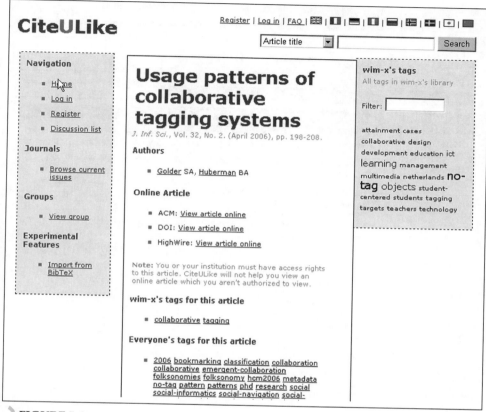

FIGURE 5-6
Example of bookmark in CiteULike

Flickr (www.flickr.com) is a slightly different take on tagging and social bookmarking activities, because it is a tagging and sharing system designed specifically for images. Flickr users upload personal images and photos into their Flickr account and then tag them. Privacy levels can be set with each photo so that some can be shared with the world, some are private to the owner, and others are shared with friends by invitation only. Flickr provides tools for resizing, rotating, and organizing the images. Developed by Ludicorp in 2002, Flickr was acquired by Yahoo! in March 2005. As of September 2006, Flickr was hosting 214 million photos for its 4 million users (Whelan 2006).

In the same vein as Flickr is YouTube (www.youtube.com), a sharing and social tagging site for videos. Founded in February 2005, YouTube was

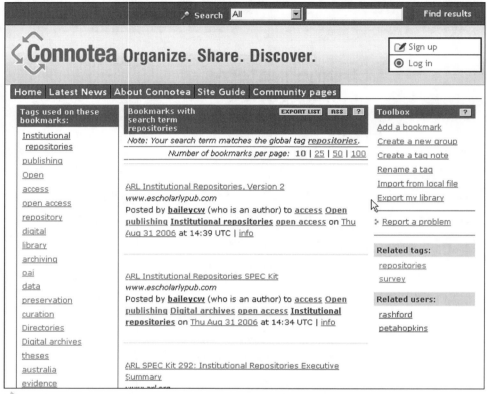

FIGURE 5-7
Bookmarks in Connotea tagged with "repositories"

designed as a social space where people could upload, tag, and share their personal videos. YouTube has proved to be immensely popular as a host for home videos, amateur films, taped performances, and recordings of outrageous stunts, pranks, and escapades. As with the other tagging services discussed thus far, YouTube's appeal comes from the social aspects of the service. In addition to uploading, tagging, and sharing videos, users can join and create video interest groups, which can form around a YouTube "artist" or genre of videos.

How popular is YouTube? According to an October 2006 article in *Forbes*, 100 million videos are viewed and 65,000 added to YouTube every day, with more than 35 million unique visitors per month (Woolley 2006, 100). It is this astonishing web traffic that prompted Google to purchase YouTube for $1.6 billion when it was a mere nineteen months old.

A tagging and social bookmarking service much closer to home is LibraryThing (www.librarything.com). Created by Tim Spalding, LibraryThing is a place for people to organize and tag books. LibraryThing pulls its book data from Amazon.com and the publicly accessible catalogs of forty-five libraries worldwide, including the Library of Congress. You simply search for a book by its author, title, or ISBN. Once found, just click on the "Add to your catalog" button and LibraryThing puts the book's bibliographic information and a copy of the book cover into your virtual library. (See fig. 5-8.)

As with the other social bookmarking services, the real value of Library-Thing comes from sharing and comparing your personal digital book collection with others. With 86,900 users and more than 6.1 million books, there are plenty of data from which to create a personalized recommendation service called "Pssst!" Moreover, there are numerous user groups that have formed around similar reading interests, including the group "Librarians who LibraryThing," which in early October 2006 was the largest group, with 846 members.

One interesting way the content tagged within a social bookmarking system can be expressed is through a "tag cloud"—a visual representation of a tag's frequency of use. The larger and bolder the font, the greater use a tag has. In the example from CiteULike in figure 5-9, the bold tags "clustering,"

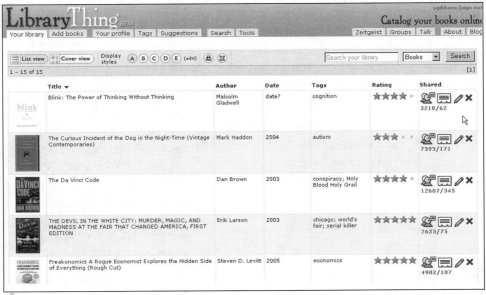

FIGURE 5-8
Author's collection in LibraryThing

"evolution," "learning," and "model" are currently the most popular, followed by those with large font sizes, including "design," "development," and "economics." Just from a quick glance at this tag cloud, it is possible to get an overview of the types of materials being collected by the users of CiteULike. The users have strong interests in the sciences, particularly biology and medicine, as well as mathematics and computer science. Almost all social bookmarking systems, including Connotea and Flickr, employ tag clouds.

Folksonomy

Tagging and social bookmarking empower the average user to do something that once was a task reserved for professionals, particularly library catalogers. With these new technologies, "users have been empowered to determine their own cataloging needs" (Kroski 2005), and it is here that tagging becomes a controversial issue for libraries. As Kroski explains,

> the wisdom of crowds, the hive mind, and the collective intelligence are doing what heretofore only expert catalogers, information architects and website authors have done. They are categorizing and organizing the Internet and determining the user experience, and it's working. (2005)

Moreover, not only are large numbers of people tagging, but they appear to be enjoying it and finding it useful.

Everyone's Tags
Most active tags on CiteULike

Filter:

algorithm analysis and architecture attention bayesian bioinformatics brain cancer classification **clustering** collaboration communication community complexity conservation control data database design detection development distributed dna docking drosophila dynamic dynamics economics education eeg emergence energy engineering **evolution** expression feedback fmri function gender gene genetics genome geometry graph hci history human hypertext information interaction knowledge language **learning** management memory method methodology methods microarray mobile **model**

FIGURE 5-9
Cloud tag from CiteULike

The arguments against tagging and social bookmarking by "nonprofessionals" center around the imprecise nature of the work and the general lack of quality control. Library cataloging is done within the framework of precise rules, the Anglo-American Cataloguing Rules (AACR), using a finite vocabulary such as the Library of Congress Subject Headings (LCSH). Tagging, however, has no such rules or restrictions. Folksonomy, the combination of the words "folksy" and "taxonomy," is the term used to denote the uncontrolled vocabulary used in tagging.

Another important difference between library cataloging and tagging is in who is doing the work. Library cataloging is the assignment of metadata to a collection on behalf of the actual users. The catalogers are acting as proxies for the actual users, the library patrons, in this activity. Tagging, however, is done by nonprofessional taggers, who are themselves the end users of the collection. In the library context this would be akin to library patrons, instead of professional catalogers, assigning subject headings to books.

These fundamental differences between tagging and formal library cataloging have given rise to quite a lively debate on the benefits of each. On the side of tagging is the fact that folksonomies, unlike formal taxonomies, "are current and capture the rapid changes in the popular world where terms and concepts change and evolve" (Gordon-Murnane 2006, 30). For example, although you can find numerous resources tagged with the term "Web 2.0," this is not an approved Library of Congress subject heading. Most of us would think that "cooking" would be an approved Library of Congress search term, but "cookery" is actually the official category term. It can take years for the approved library taxonomies to adjust and reflect changes in society, politics, and scholarship; folksonomies adjust in "real time."

Unlike library cataloging, tagging is inclusive (Gordon-Murnane 2006). Anyone can tag and be a part of a social bookmarking community; there are no monetary costs, no skill or educational requirements. And the freedom of tags ensures that they are reflective of all users, because they can "include everyone's vocabulary and reflect everyone's needs without cultural, social, or political bias" (Kroski 2005). There is no right or wrong way to tag, because tagging is first and foremost about meeting one's personal needs.

Another benefit of tagging, folksonomies, and social bookmarking is that they engender community (Kroski 2005). Although a physical library collection can, and should, do the same, the community is usually limited to those within the immediate geographic locale. In the case of an academic library, the community is restricted even further to just those affiliated with the academic institution. The taggers, on the other hand, are not restricted by geographic boundaries or academic affiliation. Anyone is welcome, and thus a strong sense of community develops. Moreover, the patrons of an academic library are primarily the users of the collection, but not the builders of the collection. Consequently, the relationship a patron forms with the collection is not quite as personal. On the other hand, the users of a tagged collection in a social bookmarking service are also the builders of that collection.

Since tags are applied by the actual users of the content, they "reflect the terms and concepts of the users of the information, rather than the creators" (Gordon-Murnane 2006, 30). For example, the Library of Congress cataloging record includes four subject headings for Thomas L. Friedman's best seller *The World Is Flat:* "Diffusion of innovations," "Information society," "Globalization—Economic aspects," and "Globalization—Social aspects." Although these may be accurate characterizations of the author's overall intent for the book, actual readers of the book remember it quite differently and in individualistic ways. Personally, I would tag Friedman's text with words such as "Globalization," "India," "China," and "Outsourcing," because these are the aspects of the book that most struck a chord with me. I find that I am not alone, for these are some of the same tags LibraryThing users have applied to this book.[4]

In other ways, library cataloging and formal taxonomies can be superior to tagging and folksonomies. Because of the absence of formal rules and controlled vocabulary, tagging can be quite messy and imprecise. For example, tags are limited to single words and therefore cannot support phrases. Taggers have tried to get around this limitation by creating compound words such as "newyorkcity," "new_york_city," and "new-york-city." But since there is no accepted standard for creating such compound phrases, there can be a multiplicity of tags with the same meaning. This, in turn, impacts the comprehensiveness of retrieval. For example, to retrieve all resources with some connection to New York City, you would have to search across all the possible tags for New York City, including nyc, newyorkcity, new_york_city, ny_city, new-york-city, and more.

Plurals create a similar problem. Again, there is no accepted, widely practiced standard to dictate whether tags should be singular ("dog") or plural ("dogs"), and consequently this decision is left to the preferences of the tagger. Moreover, there is no automatic clustering of synonyms and related words (e.g., "dogs," "canine," "pooch") or any way to disambiguate homonyms such as "bill" as a legislative bill, a playbill, a dollar bill, a bill of goods, or short for William. Add to all of this the reality that people frequently misspell and mistype, and folksonomic taggings appear quite chaotic. Or, as Golder and Huberman more eloquently put it, "Collective tagging . . . has the potential to exacerbate the problems associated with the fuzziness of linguistics and cognitive boundaries" (2006, 201).

Another criticism of tagging and folksonomies is that they are much too personal. When Golder and Huberman (2006) conducted an analysis of del.icio.us tags, they found several common tag functions. Tags identify what (or who) something is about, what it is (e.g., article, book, blog), who owns it, and its qualities or characteristics (e.g., funny, stupid, inspirational). Only some of the tags they analyzed had value to anyone beyond the actual tagger, such as a photo tagged "my_house" or a book tagged "to_read." Remember, however, that the primary function of tags is to help "keep found things found" at a personal level; the main value of a tag is to the tagger herself. This would suggest, however, that the value of social bookmarking systems is diminished when there is an abundance of highly personalized tags.

Early detractors of social bookmarking services believed that, without a fixed taxonomy, the folksonomy that emerged would consist of nothing more than personalized terms used only once. But Guy and Tonkin (2006) found that single-use tags were less common than they had expected. A study of Flickr and del.icio.us tags found that only 10–15% of the sample tags were single use; the vast majority of tags were found to have a shared value. Similarly, the tags used in Connotea suggest the emergence of a shared user vocabulary. Lund et al. (2005) studied 3,359 unique Connotea tags and found that 14% were shared by two or more users, 6% were shared by three or more, and 3% were shared by four or more. They concluded that the distribution of tag use follows a "classic power law," or, to use the popular term coined by Chris Anderson (2006), tags have a "long tail."

Sinha (2005) explains the attraction of tagging as opposed to categorizing (e.g., cataloging) in terms of cognitive psychology. Categorizing requires one to decide which category to place an item into—for example, which of the Library of Congress subject headings to assign to a book. Tagging, on the other hand, requires a person only to produce "semantic associations" for an object, such as "book," "science fiction," and "favorite author." The former requires far more cognitive processing, because a person must make a discrete decision, which can cause what Sinha describes as "analysis-paralysis." Tagging eliminates the need to make a choice and removes the fear of making the wrong choice. Sinha concludes that a primary reason for the popularity of tagging is that "it taps into the existing cognitive process without adding much cognitive cost," and I think we can all appreciate that.

When compared to library cataloging, tagging is by far the cheaper and quicker activity. Tagging requires no training or resources, whereas an expert library cataloger can require years of formal training and practice as well as cataloging software and reference tools. Overall, when compared with formal library cataloging, "folksonomy data is much noisier but also more flexible, more abundant and far cheaper" (Hammond et al. 2005).

The debate between tagging and cataloging and the use of folksonomies and taxonomies need not be an either-or proposition. As Crawford suggests, these are false dichotomies. There are pros and cons for each, as well as situations where one outvalues the other. After weighing both sides of the debate, he concludes that "tagging isn't going away, nor should it. Neither are formal taxonomies and classification/cataloging systems going away. There's room for both, and there should be ways to use each to enrich the other" (2006, 3).

Tagging and Social Bookmarking in Academic Libraries

Academic libraries can use tagging, social bookmarking, and folksonomies to support student research skills and build a sense of community around the libraries' collections in a variety of ways.

In several respects, tagging and social bookmarking are new organizational tools for conducting library research. One way to think of them is as a more efficient, modern alternative to the once ubiquitous 3 x 5 note cards for keeping track of citations. Note cards are easily misplaced; the important bookmarks, citations, and notations saved in a social bookmarking service are stored online in a way that is not easily lost.

Because social bookmarking can in fact be an efficient research tool to help students "keep found things found," academic libraries should do more to promote and support their use. For example, the bookmarklets of popular social bookmarking systems like del.icio.us should be added to the Internet browser of the library's public computer terminals to make it easier for students to use them. The University of Pennsylvania Libraries have gone a great deal farther in their support of social bookmarking. Recognizing the value of social bookmarking, they created PennTags (tags.library.upenn.edu), a local social bookmarking service designed specifically for the university community. In addition to providing a useful research tool, PennTags supports the formation of discipline-based communities on campus by providing a mechanism through which the common interests among students become visible (Allen and Winkler 2006). Using the university's central authentication system, students and faculty can create PennTags accounts and begin saving their bookmarks. A PennTags bookmarklet places the PennTags tool a single click away. In addition, "Add to PennTags" buttons are in the libraries' catalog and

SFX OpenURL resolver so that students can easily add resources into their PennTags accounts.

By October 2006, fourteen months after its launch, there were 8,972 bookmarks by 582 unique users in PennTags. The bookmarks contained more than 7,300 unique tags, which were used more than 26,700 times. Approximately one-quarter of the resources bookmarked came from the university libraries' catalog, demonstrating that students do still use the catalog. Many of the users of PennTags are creating annotated bibliographies. Some are quite small, others both comprehensive and impressive, such as "The Consequences of Media Conglomerate Breakups," "Indian Travel Literature," and "Business Area Studies." These bibliographies demonstrate how social bookmarking systems can be used to create subject guides, course guides, and other resources that can make use of an annotated bibliography format.

Another social bookmarking system, similar to PennTags, is H2O Playlist (h2obeta.law.harvard.edu/home.do), created by the Berkman Center for Internet and Society at Harvard Law School. H2O is available for anyone to use, without a fee. More important, the source code for the system has been made open source, distributed under the GNU General Public License.[5] Consequently, any academic library can create a local version of H2O Playlist for their local community of users.

An interesting by-product of PennTags is its tag cloud. As Etches-Johnson explains, the tag cloud is a "snapshot of user behavior within the University of Pennsylvania community" (2006, 58). As of late 2006, PennTag users had high levels of interest in business area studies, copyright, film, and transportation. The tag cloud could become a useful collection development tool as new interests within the community begin to emerge through the cloud.

Another way to use a tag cloud is as a more efficient alternative to scouring the search logs of a library's catalog and website to discern local user patterns and research interests. Dave Pattern, library systems manager at the University of Huddersfield, has demonstrated how this could work by creating a tag cloud using the most popular search terms from his online catalog over six months. He has posted the result on Flickr and on his blog, *"Self-plagiarism is style."*[6]

Tag clouds could also be used to provide a visual representation of a library's collection. Using subject headings in the catalog, a cloud tag could be created to give a user a quick, graphic overview of the strengths of a library's collection. More refined cloud tags could be created for particular subject areas, such as history monographs and serials, which could then be added to the history subject guide. With one glance, for example, a user could immediately see that the library's history collection is far stronger in Southeast Asian history than African history. Again, Dave Pattern of Huddersfield gives us a glimpse of what this might look like, by creating a cloud tag of subject keywords with more than ten bibliographic records in the online catalog.[7]

Although social bookmarking appears to fit easily within the scope of academic libraries as an emerging research tool, for some libraries tagging can be a less comfortable fit. But why not let your community of users add tags to supplement the subject headings in your online catalog? John Blyberg (2006) makes the following argument in his blog post about the trust relationships that can develop between users and their libraries:

> Something like OPAC tagging (which will, eventually, be in the canon of online library service) is a terribly hard sell (I know, I've tried) because the response is, "we're going to let our users do *what?*" I think there are two reasons why this is an entirely inappropriate response. First, it obviates the notion of radical trust between library and patron. Second, it presupposes that social OPACs and authoritative OPACs are mutually exclusive. Both of these fallacies in an argument against OPAC tagging will, in time, deteriorate as long as some of us continue to push the issue. They will eventually disappear because any resistance to OPAC tagging, or social OPACs in general, is not based on any reasoned argument.

While many libraries are debating the pros and cons of adding user tags to their catalogs, others are simply doing it. Again, the University of Pennsylvania Libraries are on the forefront. For any resource from the libraries' catalog that has been tagged or annotated in PennTags, that information has been copied into the library catalog and appended to the bottom of the item record. Plymouth State University's experimental WPopac places the tagging feature right into the user interface of the OPAC.[8] The tags themselves link to the blog search engine Technorati, which displays the results of a Technorati search on that tag term. By these means, the WPopac is no longer just a catalog of items owned by Plymouth State University; instead, it is the jumping-off point for relevant resources from across the Web.

The tools of Web 2.0 provide academic libraries with great opportunities to both engage Net Generation students and support their academic endeavors. The contrasts will only deepen between a library with a Web 1.0 presence and the real competitors leveraging Web 2.0 tools. It is time to not just theorize about the concept of Library 2.0 but make it a reality, before we are just too late.

NOTES

1. See, for example, http://pim.ischool.washington.edu/index.htm or http://chandler.osafoundation.org.
2. Quoted from http://www.citeulike.org/faq/all.adp.
3. Download at http://sf.net/projects/connotea/.
4. See, for example, http://www.librarything.com/work/836&book=7827074.
5. Explanation and link to source code at http://h2obeta.law.harvard.edu/help.do#code.
6. See http://www.flickr.com/photos/davepattern/323769216/and http://www.daveyp.com/blog/index.php/archives/147/.
7. See http://www.daveyp.com/blog/stuff/subjects.html.
8. See http://www.plymouth.edu/library/opac/record/1325594.

CHAPTER SIX

The Net Generation as Communicators

THUS FAR, WE HAVE SEEN HOW TECHNOLOGY has changed the way Net Geners play games, keep current (RSS), write and coauthor (blogs and wikis), and keep found things found (tagging and social bookmarking). But the differences do not end there. Technology is also transforming the way Net Generation students communicate.

Cell Phones

Cell phones have become an essential part of the Net Generation's accoutrement. Nearly half of U.S. teens today (45%) own a cell phone (Lenhart, Madden, and Hitlin 2005, ii). Among college students the penetration is nearly exhaustive. A recent EDUCAUSE report found that nearly 82% of college students in this country own a cell phone. By gender, this breaks down to 84.7% of female and 77.7% of male students (Kvavik 2005, 7.3).

The consequences of the ubiquity of cell phones on college campuses are felt in many ways. For example, cell phones have made dorm room "landlines" nearly obsolete. Although this can take some burden off the campus telecommunications department, it has caused many of our office long-distance phone bills to skyrocket. Students' cell phone numbers have become part of their identities, in much the same way their e-mail addresses have. Consequently, when they come to campus they have little or no incentive to exchange their cell phones for local phone numbers, because they want their friends and family to continue to know how to contact them. What this means for an academic campus, however, is that the vast majority of the students who live on campus are reachable only by a long-distance phone call. A ten-digit phone number with area code is rapidly replacing the local seven-digit phone number as the norm.

Another consequence of the high level of cell phone ownership among Net Generation students is that they can more easily than past generations keep in contact with their hometown friends, family, and, in particular, parents. Most cell carriers have some sort of family-share plan in which calls between the members of a family are free. Students are now able to call their parents, and vice versa, without hesitation or worry about cost. This has transformed the weekly ritual of calling home from the dorm into a daily, if not more frequent, event.

A two-year study of undergraduates conducted by the University of Rochester River Campus Libraries included a reflective exercise in which the students drew and recounted the activities they undertook from the time a research paper was assigned until it was submitted. A common feature of these reflections was students consulting their parents about the assignment. This new phenomenon appears to be the result of several factors. For one, with each incoming freshman class the percentage of students who have at least one parent who attended college increases (National Center for Education Statistics 2005, table 29-3). It is only natural for a student to seek advice from parents who are familiar with the college academic experience.

The close involvement of parents in their child's college activities can also be seen as an extension of the parental sheltering Net Generation students experienced in their youth. As these students come to campus, in many ways so too do their hovering, "helicopter parents." A 2006 survey of parents of college students revealed that 81.6% of parents rated their level of involvement with their college-bound children to be either "more involved" or "much more involved" than they experienced when in college (College Parents of America 2006).

Another factor seems to be the ease with which students communicate with their parents because of cell phones. Cell phones have removed the inconvenience and cost that were once barriers to calling home from the dorm. So why not call Mom or Dad to ask for advice about a research paper topic?

Many of us pre–Net Geners use cell phones on a regular basis. Where our experience differs from Net Geners' is in the fact that they use cell phones for far more than just making phone calls. With most cell phones you can surf the Internet, read your e-mail, take and send pictures, record and watch video clips, listen to MP3 audio files, edit Microsoft Word and Excel documents, update your appointment calendar, get directions from a GPS navigator, and receive your morning wake-up alarm. Digital cameras, PDAs, MP3 players, and cell phones are all rapidly converging into a single, portable device, and Net Geners are thus far the most adept at leveraging the full potential of their cell phones.

Text messaging was one of the first cell phone expansions beyond basic, core telephony. Referred to as SMS (short message service), this service is available on nearly all cell phones. Essentially SMS is little more than the transmission of short text messages over cell phones. Initially SMS messages had to be typed on the number pad of the phone with its corresponding associated letters. For example, writing the word "yes" would require three hits of the 9 key, two hits of the 3 key, and four hits of the 7 key. Recently miniature keyboards have been added to the design of some higher-end cell phones. Even so, the mechanics of writing complete, grammatically correct sentences can be taxing when you are typing with only your thumbs on a seemingly microscopic keyboard.

The difficulty of typing messages on cell phones has led to the development of a more efficient, written form of the English language, called SMS language, txt, and chatspeak, among others. In this emerging language, definite and indefinite articles are eliminated, "unnecessary" vowels are dropped, and phonetic spelling is the norm. For example, "see you later" becomes "cu l8r," which eliminates more than half of the required keystrokes. For many more examples of SMS language, see Wikipedia's alphabetical list of SMS abbreviations.[1]

Another way to communicate by cell phone texting is with emoticons (a combination of the words "emotion" and "icons"). These are short sequences of keyboard characters that represent sideways facial expressions and are intended to convey emotions. Beginning with the simple happy :-) and sad face :-(emoticons have been developed to express a wide range of emotions, including worried :-S surprised = O and very sad (:-\. There are many lists of emoticons on the Internet including a helpful one in the *ComputerUser High-Tech Dictionary.*[2]

The cell phone is not, however, the only device on which to use the SMS language and emoticons. This language has moved on to what is today the most frequently used form of technology-based communication among teens, instant messaging (Lenhart, Madden, and Hitlin 2005, iii).

Instant Messaging

Instant messaging (IM), also known as online chat, is the nearly synchronous communication through short text messages over the Internet. IM is accomplished via a software program that is loaded onto the user's computer, such as AOL Instant Messenger (AIM), Yahoo! Messenger, or MSN Messenger. Each user picks a unique "screen name." These names vary from a derivation of one's own name (my AIM name is "susanlgibbons") to something unrecognizable such as "tiptoptom." As you identify people with whom you want to chat, you exchange screen names and add them to your IM "buddy list." A buddy can start a chat with you at any time, but non-buddies must first virtually request and obtain permission to start a chat. Your IM software keeps track of your buddies' availability and can give you a visual and auditory alert if a buddy's status changes.

IM services are generally exclusive, so that a person is restricted to chatting with only those people who use the same service, such as AIM. Some cross-platform IM systems, such as Trillian, have, however, been developed to allow chatting across all of the major IM systems.[3]

In 2005 the Pew Internet and American Life Project found that 16 million American teens were using IM. Almost half (48%) of them said they used it daily, with almost 30% using it several times a day (Lenhart, Madden, and Hitlin 2005, 16). In another study, 40.5% of college students reported using IM daily, with another 29.7% using it hourly (Vanden Boogart 2006, 30). The Pew report examined duration of IM use as well. On a typical day, 27% used IM for less than 30 minutes, 37% for a half hour to an hour, 24% between one and two hours a day, and 11% for more than two hours a day (Lenhart, Madden, and Hitlin 2005, 17). This high usage led the researchers to conclude that "instant messaging has become the digital communication backbone of teens' daily lives" (Lenhart, Madden, and Hitlin 2005, iii).

IM use differs quite markedly along generational lines, in particular compared to e-mail use. For 46% of Net Geners, IM is used more frequently than e-mail. This number falls quite precipitously to only 18% for Generation X, and the percentages get even smaller for the older generations (Shiu and Lenhart 2004, iii). In a recent Pew focus group, the teens said that "they view email as something you use to talk to 'old people,' 'institutions,' or 'to send complex instructions to large groups'" (Lenhart, Madden, and Hitlin 2005, ii). When most of us weren't looking, e-mail became old-fashioned.

As many of us have observed, communicating via IM is rarely an isolated activity. "Notably, close to half of instant messaging teens (45%) say that when they use IM they engage in several separate IM conversations at the same time on a daily or almost daily basis" (Lenhart, Madden, and Hitlin 2005, 22). Some use IM while watching television, talking on the phone, writing papers, surfing the Internet, and playing video games. Pauses in an IM conversation are expected when a person needs to direct all of her attention to another activity, such as answering the phone; she will resume the IM conversation when she can.

The universe of people with whom teens use IM to communicate is, however, surprisingly small. Nearly two-thirds of users regularly use IM with only one to five people. Only 9% of IM users regularly communicate with more than ten people (Shiu and Lenhart 2004, v). Those people with whom they do use IM tend to be friends who do not live nearby or who go to a different school, such as a college student staying in touch with his friends from high school (Lenhart, Madden, and Hitlin 2005, 23). IM does not replace in-person relationships. Instead, it helps to sustain them when face-to-face interaction is just not possible.

The most popular IM programs, such as AIM and MSN Messenger, include functionality that allows users to personalize their IM identity. For example, an IM user can associate an icon with his screen name. The icon could be a photo, drawing, or other graphic representation. The degree of personalization is, however, rather limited. Those who seek a more robust form of self-expression, as well as keep in touch with friends, turn to the social networking services of Facebook and MySpace.

Social Networking Services

Facebook (www.facebook.com) was launched in February 2004 as a "social utility that helps people better understand the world around them," according to the website. The service was created by Mark Zuckerberg when he was a sophomore at Harvard University, in order to create the online equivalent of a college yearbook. The success and popularity of Facebook on the Harvard campus led Zuckerberg and his colleagues to expand it (Carnevale 2006). Today, nearly anyone can join Facebook.

Facebook is made up of discrete networks, such as colleges, high schools, and companies. A person can join a network only if officially affiliated with it, such as a student at a college, which is verifiable by the student's valid e-mail address from that institution. Once you establish an account, you can then create a profile, which reflects you and your interests. (See fig. 6-1.)

The depth of your Facebook profile is up to you. You can add photos and contact information as well as personal facts such as your birth date, hometown, marital status, favorite music and books, and work and educational background. A nice feature of Facebook is called "Pulse," which aggregates the "favorites" of a network, such as the University of Rochester, and compares them with all Facebook users. This is a terrific tool for getting a better sense of the interests of your institution's student body. At the University of Rochester, in early December 2006 the Beatles, Coldplay, and Dave Matthews Band were the popular music groups; *Fight Club* and *Garden State* the most popular movies; and *Family Guy* and *Grey's Anatomy* the favorite television programs.

As you make friends who also have Facebook profiles, you can exchange permission to add one another to your Facebook "friends" list. For privacy purposes, it is only members of your network and official friends who can see

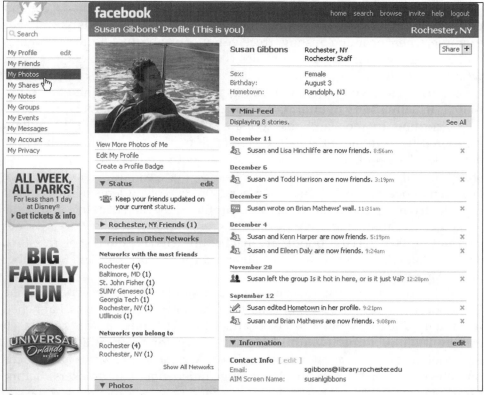

> **FIGURE 6-1**
> Author's Facebook profile

the details of your full profile. Another way to discover friends is by joining groups that range in topics from "Class of 2005 Alumni" and "Chem132 Lab" to "I Like to Pretend Rochester is Hogwarts," which had 175 members in early December 2006.

There are many ways to communicate and keep in touch with friends through Facebook. "Messages" work like private e-mail, except that you have to log on to Facebook to receive them. You can also leave public messages by writing them on a friend's "virtual wall," which is in some ways akin to graffiti. Another communication feature of Facebook is called "poke." When you poke a friend, it simply tells her that you poked her, a sort of virtual nudge. Although this may seem like a pointless feature, Facebook reports that on Saturday, December 2, 2006, "833 Rochester people poked each other."

Much of the activity of Facebook is social, focused heavily on dating and getting dates. But Facebook serves other important student needs as well. For example, when incoming freshmen receive notice of who their dorm roommates will be, reading their Facebook profiles is often a useful way to get a sense of who they really are, common interests, and the likelihood of compatibility. If your friend sets you up on a blind date, you need not be so blind, because there is usually plenty of information to be found on her Facebook profile.

According to the Facebook website, there are more than 12 million registered users in more than 40,000 regional, work, college, and high school networks. Facebook is immensely popular with college students. A case study of four universities found that 94.4% of students had a Facebook page (Vanden Boogart 2006, 27). In September 2005, 85% of students in the colleges represented in Facebook had a Facebook profile. Sixty percent of those students logged on to Facebook daily, 85% once a week, and 93% at least once a month (Arrington 2005). It is this popularity that has attracted the interest of investors, such as Yahoo!, which made a $1 billion bid for Facebook in late September 2006 (Agrawal 2006).

MySpace (www.myspace.com) has many similarities to Facebook. Unlike Facebook, though, MySpace is not based on the concept of networks. Launched in January 2004 by Tom Anderson and Chris DeWolfe, it was purchased in July 2005 by Rupert Murdoch's News Corp for $580 million. Whereas Facebook was created as an online yearbook, MySpace has always had a focus on self-promotion. "From the beginning, independent filmmakers, actors, aspiring comedians and, particularly, unsigned rock bands have used the site to promote themselves—so many that MySpace became known, not quite accurately, as a music site" (Williams 2005). A MySpace profile has become the primary marketing vehicle for many performers, who use it to post music files, announce upcoming performance venues, and keep their fans informed and excited about their success.

MySpace has more than 106 million registered users (more than ten times the size of Facebook), with approximately 230,000 new accounts created daily. In June 2005, MySpace surpassed Google in web traffic, averaging 1 billion visitors daily (Sellers 2006).

As with Facebook, MySpace is built on the concept of individual profiles. Your profile can include pictures, information about your interests, schools, marital status, and so on. Music and video files can be added to a profile as well. Friends are added into your network through mutual agreement. You can IM via the MySpace chat system with friends who are logged on. Friends can also add comments to your public bulletin board and send messages to one another. (See fig. 6-2.) All profiles come with a free blog account, which encourages

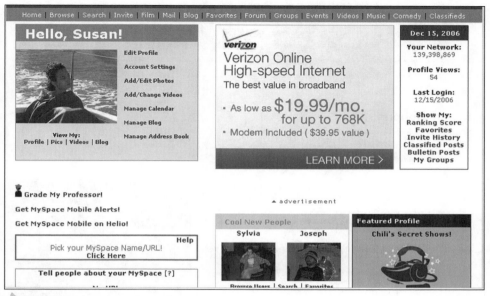

FIGURE 6-2
Author's MySpace profile

all users to give blogging a try. And recently MySpace added a "Grade my professor" system, which works in a similar fashion to Ratemyprofessor.com, so that student members can easily share comments about their professors.

MySpace and Facebook are certainly the most popular social networking systems at present, but there are many others. Examples include Bebo (www .bebo.com), popular in the United Kingdom; Friendster (www.friendster.com), one of the oldest social networking sites; and LinkedIn (www.linkedin.com), which focuses on the networking of professional relationships. (See fig. 6-3.)

Academic Library Uses of New Communication Technologies

There are several ways an academic library can leverage the potential of cell phones, IM, and social networking services such as Facebook and MySpace to further its mission. In spite of the high percentage of college students who have cell phones, academic libraries do not always do enough to communicate with students through that medium. For example, we need to make it easier and more convenient for students to use their cell phones to call the reference desk. For this to happen, the reference desk phone number must be "plastered"

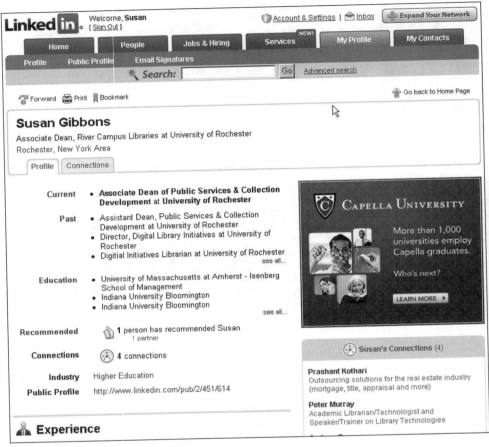

FIGURE 6-3
Author's LinkedIn profile

all about the library, book stacks, campus, and university website, and not just posted on the library home page and campus phone directory. Another approach is to end a bibliographic instruction session by asking the students to take out their cell phones and program in your office or reference desk phone number.

During the 2006 freshman move-in day at the University of Rochester campus, the River Campus Libraries placed a trivia question into the freshman "welcome bag." While the students waited anxiously in their cars with their parents for their turn to move into the dorms, they would naturally sort through the bag of goodies to see what was there. The libraries' trivia question was about the Beatles, in order to get the parents involved too. A student who thought she knew the answer was invited to call the reference desk, and if her answer was correct she was entered into a drawing for an iPod. If she did not know the answer, she could call the reference desk, get the answer, and also be entered into the drawing. The purpose was to get the student to call the reference desk from her cell phone, in the hopes that she would then add the phone number to her cell phone directory. Essentially it is a matter of socializing the idea with students that cell phones are a perfectly appropriate and welcomed way to interact with the library.

Prensky (2005) has written about the many ways cell phones can be used in education. He points to the popularity of cell phones as a tool for learning foreign languages in China and Japan. The company Go Test Go (www .gotestgo.com) has developed testing software for cell phones, including SAT preparation, English vocabulary, and even a Canadian vehicle safety quiz. Prensky also points to the example of Minute Man National Historical Park in Concord, Massachusetts, which provides guided voice tours over visitors' cell phones. Academic libraries could model similar cell phone–based services for students, such as audio library tours and subscriptions to foreign-language and test preparation content for delivery over students' phones. Medical libraries have been on the forefront of providing content to their patrons through PDAs. The convergence of PDAs and cell phones means that this same content, such as that found in the *Physician's Desk Reference* and *PubMed,* is now available via cell phones. Chemical Abstracts Service is preparing a database of molecular images that can be accessed via cell phone, and we should expect the pool of phone-ready content to expand.

Cell phones can also be a convenient way to get information pushed out to students using SMS. For example, Penn State University recently launched a text-messaging service called PSUTXT. Registered users of the service can presently sign up to receive text messages about campus emergencies, sports, and concert information, but the breadth of information is expected to expand. The service has been far more popular with students than the university administration expected, with more than a thousand subscribers in the first three weeks of service (Carnevale 2006). As more campuses adopt SMS as a communication means, academic libraries should be ready to supply relevant and appropriate content, such as changes in library hours and notices of special library events.

"Voting" is another increasingly common way to use text messaging. For example, the popular television program *American Idol* solicits viewers to vote for their favorite contestants via telephone or SMS. During the fourth season of *American Idol,* viewers sent more than 41.5 million text messages. Text messaging has been used to vote in local elections in the United Kingdom,[4] for viewer surveys by ESPN, and to determine which videos should be played on

MTV. Academic libraries can use SMS voting as well, by inviting students to use it to indicate their preferences about services, to RSVP for library events, or to share thoughts about a recent renovation.

As more and more people turn to their cell phones to surf the Web, information and content providers need to design alternate versions of their websites that are appropriate for display on small cell phone screens. The small-screen version of the Google website pushes the simple search box into the top left corner of the screen so that the user does not have to scroll across to the center of the screen to find it. Palm has developed something similar as the default website for cell phones built on the Palm operating system. ABC and BBC News, Sports Illustrated, and Orbitz all have alternate websites designed specifically for the small-screen market.[5] For an academic library, such a redesign would require paring down the website to just a few basic functions (e.g., catalog search, circulation renewals, staff directory) and eliminating all unnecessary graphics and images; Western Kentucky University's library is one such example.[6]

IM has become the most frequently used form of online communication for students, and consequently one academic libraries should take seriously. At a higher education conference in 2002, Brown made the following observation:

> Most people of a certain age probably don't do IM because we didn't grow up with it. But if the game we're talking about is amplifying your ability to socially construct your understanding, IM may have a significant role in learning environments. (2002, 62)

Avoiding IM means shutting off an avenue for students to engage and converse with their libraries.

Some academic libraries are addressing the increase in IM popularity with the introduction of virtual reference and chat services. Often the software applications libraries use are commercial, vendor-based products such as LiveAssistance and Docutek VRLplus. The cited advantages of the vendor-based chat programs are automatic statistical tracking, queuing of simultaneous chat requests, co-browsing, and requiring users to complete a form before chatting (Ward and Kern 2006, 420). But the mounting evidence suggests that these advantageous features of the vendor-based chat are far outweighed by their disadvantages, which Lupien (2006) refers to as a "minefield of obstacles." For example, there are browser and operating system incompatibilities with almost all virtual reference software. Moreover, virtual reference systems work by opening a new browser window, which requires the user to disable his pop-up blocker, firewall, or both, and this places his computer at risk to viruses and worms. These barriers can often be a deterrent to use or make for a problematic experience when used. After studying the problems associated with vendor-based virtual reference software, Lupien (2006) concluded that there was no one commercial virtual reference solution that could eliminate all of these problems. More important, the use of vendor chat for virtual reference systems is library-centric rather than user-centric. "Forcing users to extend outside their comfort zone and asking them to use software communication tools they are unfamiliar with does not necessarily create a formula for reaching the broadest user base possible" (Ward and Kern 2006, 428).

One solution seems obvious. Libraries can turn to the free IM software the students are already using, such as AOL Instant Messenger, MSN Messenger, and Yahoo! Messenger. Although the library would lose some of the advantages of the vendor-based software, including co-browsing, it would gain the use of a chat system that is compatible with most operating systems and browsers, avoids the problems of pop-up blockers and firewalls, and is familiar to nearly the entire undergraduate student population:

> Librarians who offer IM feel that by providing IM reference, they are aligning their services with the preferred technology of an important user group [undergraduates]. IM allows patrons to use the technology that they prefer rather than forcing users to communicate with librarians using "library technology." (Lupien 2006)

The successful use of IM as a chat reference service by academic libraries can be seen at Morrisville State College (Drew 2005), the University of Illinois at Urbana-Champaign (Ward and Kern 2006), and the University of Richmond (McCulley and Reinauer 2006), among others.

Another way academic librarians can make use of the current popularity of IM is to add it to the growing list of ways students and faculty can contact the library. Public terminals in the library should have the popular IM systems loaded onto them, with the reference desk and subject librarians already programmed into the buddy list. Add your IM name to your business cards, subject and course guides, and staff directory (see fig. 6-4). Share it with students during your bibliographic instruction sessions. Generic IM accounts for the reference desks and subject libraries should be posted on the library website, along with the related e-mail and phone number, such as is done nicely at the University of Illinois at Urbana-Champaign.[7]

Just as students are heavy users of IM, they are using social networking systems at high rates, and consequently academic libraries need to pay attention. Because of its initial academic focus, Facebook seems to lend itself more as a tool for academic libraries to reach and communicate with students.

University of Rochester > River Campus Libraries > Political Science Library Research Guide (beta) >

Political Science Research

→ Ask a Librarian **Live!**
→ Search Site

Subject Librarian: Ann Marshall
Location: Rush Rhees Library
Email: amarshall@library.rochester.edu
Phone: 585-273-3451
AOL IM: AnnMMarshall
Office Hours: Thursday 4–5 pm in Rush Rhees 106
Friday 10 am–noon in Harkness 315 computer lab & by appt.

A guide to resources supporting teaching and research at the UR Political Science Dept.

- **Political Science Databases**
  Books, journal articles, data,
  legislation, policy analysis

- **World Politics by Region/Country**
  Gateway sites, Europe, Canada,
  Latin America

- **World Politics by Topic**
  International relations, constitutions,
  treaties, NGOs, political economy,
  conflict studies, human rights,
  terrorism

- **Guides and Handouts** Setting up e-
  reserves, class handouts
  ISI citation search, search tips

- **Writing Research Papers**
  Thesis statements, writing tips,
  how to quote, revise, cite

- **Guide to Political Science Data**
  ICPSR, datasets, international data,
  election results, polls

- **American Politics**
  Gateway sites, interest groups,
  parties, state and local, public policy,
  race, law, campaign finance

FIGURE 6-4
Subject guide from University of Rochester Libraries with librarian's
AOL Instant Messenger name

Brian Mathews, a librarian at Georgia Tech University, has explored the ways academic libraries can and cannot use Facebook. When he searched for the nearly 1,700 Georgia Tech mechanical engineering students in Facebook, he found more than 1,300 of them—an astounding 76%. He sent a Facebook message to each student marketing himself (as librarian) and some of the resources of the Georgia Tech Library (Mathews 2006a). Unfortunately, he later learned that this was a violation of Facebook policy (Mathews 2006c), because it was considered spamming. Although only forty-eight students responded, he believes that he was more successful than the low response rate suggests:

> For instance, I was asked to be "friends" by several students, which is a sign
> of acceptance. I also received a handful of AOL instant messages inquiring
> about journals and conference papers. Perhaps most surprisingly, however,

were the students who approached me around campus, at the student center, the gym, and even a football game, to say hello and that they had seen me on Facebook. Overall, the effort effectively helped me to expand the goal of promoting the library and my role as subject liaison. (Mathews 2006a)

Until recently, profiles could be created for nonindividuals such as libraries and academic departments, but Facebook decided to limit profiles to individuals and deleted the profiles of more than seventy libraries along with the other nonindividual profiles. This does not force librarians completely out of Facebook, but it does require us to come out from behind our institutional identities and act as individuals within Facebook.

In his blog posting "What to Do When Facebook Closes Down Your Library Storefront," Mathews (2006d) makes several great suggestions about how individual librarians can make use of Facebook:

- Join Facebook groups formed around classes that have a resource component and market your assistance.
- Partner with other departments, such as tutoring, to form groups that support the educational process.
- Use Facebook to locate students for focus groups and to gather opinions.

Other ideas include using the Facebook "flyer" feature to advertise library events and special occasions and sending tailored messages about targeted library services to appropriate Facebook groups.

Social networking services such as Facebook and MySpace are changing rapidly, and we are only just beginning to explore and realize the potential they hold for furthering the missions of academic libraries. With 60%, 75%, or perhaps even more of our students using these social networking services as a communication venue, we just cannot ignore them.

NOTES

1. At http://en.wikipedia.org/wiki/List_of_SMS_abbreviations.
2. At http://www.computeruser.com/resources/dictionary/emoticons.html.
3. See more about Trillian at http://www.ceruleanstudios.com.
4. http://news.bbc.co.uk/2/hi/uk_news/politics/1802956.stm.
5. See these examples at http://www.google.com/pda, http://mobile.palm.com/us/, http://wireless.go.com/wireless/abcnews/xhtml/index/, http://news.bbc.co.uk/text_only.stm, http://mobile.cnn.com/xhtml/en/us/si/i.html, and http://mobile.orbitz.com.
6. See http://www.wku.edu/Library/tip/pda/index.htm.
7. See http://www.library.uiuc.edu/askus/.

CHAPTER SEVEN

Conclusions

MOST OF THIS BOOK FOCUSES ON SOME OF THE more popular technologies in use by today's students and some specific changes academic libraries can consider to take advantage of these technologies. But the technologies Net Generation students are now using are in a constant state of flux. With that in mind, in this final chapter we take a few steps back from the specific, immediate trends to address more generally what academic libraries can do to ensure that they are continually in step with their students while fulfilling their mission to be the best in the world at serving the unique teaching, learning, and research needs of their home academic institutions by actively participating in the creation, transmission, and dissemination of knowledge.

The pace of change, particularly with technology, may seem fast now, but it will only quicken. In his prescient *Age of Spiritual Machines,* Kurweil points to two "laws" that help explain why the pace of technological development will rapidly accelerate. The first is Moore's Law on integrated circuits, posited by Gordon Moore in 1965 with a revision in 1975. Moore's Law predicts that the surface area of a transistor can be cut in half every eighteen to twenty-four months.

> The result is that every two years, you can pack twice as many transistors on an integrated chip. This doubles both the number of components on a chip as well as its speed. Since the cost of an integrated circuit is fairly constant, the implication is that every two years you can get twice as much circuitry running at twice the speed for the same price. (Kurweil 1999, 27)

What this essentially means is that for the same amount of money you can purchase a computer with twice as much computing power and speed approximately every two years.

The second law is the Law of Accelerating Returns. Kurweil explains: "As order [the opposite of chaos] exponentially increases, time exponentially speeds up (that is, the time interval between salient events grows shorter as time passes)" (1999, 30). With any kind of exponential growth, the initial growth period is slow, such as with compound interest on a savings account. But because the growth is exponential (x^2) and not arithmetic ($2x$ or $x + 2$), it accelerates at a much faster pace. The lesson here is not to take the historic pace of change to be a predictor of the future pace of change. Rather, we should assume that the future pace of change will be faster.

It is not, however, just technology that we must strive to keep abreast with. Nicholson explains that "this transformation requires that research libraries adapt rapidly not only to the breakneck pace of technology, but even more fundamentally to new information seeking and user behaviors of students and faculty alike" (2006, 10). Culturally, most academic libraries struggle to keep up with change at today's pace, which makes it difficult to imagine how we will do so as the pace of change accelerates. Ours is a risk-adverse, generally conservative occupation. Consequently, our reactions to change come quite slowly, yet deliberately and with purposeful intentions. Proposals for new services, for example, are formed and vetted by committee, with all potential alternatives exhaustively explored over many months. We strive to reach a point at which all the potential outcomes of a change in service are known and the results are largely predictable. I am sure we can all find evidence of a proposed change—such as moving to an approval plan, purchasing shelf-ready books, starting a chat-based reference service, or building an institutional repository—stuck in a committee somewhere in our libraries. Unfortunately, the result is "an apparent disconnect between the culture of library organizations and that of Net Gen students" (Lippincott 2005, 13.1).

Academic libraries are not alone. They share their conservative culture with their university hosts. How long will it take before outstanding digital scholarship, such as Edward L. Ayers's Valley of the Shadow: Two Communities in the American Civil War (valley.vcdh.virginia.edu) or Morris Eaves's William Blake Archive (www.blakearchive.org/blake/), counts uniformly toward tenure in the same way a published monograph does today? Why do faculty only scratch the surface of the full functionality and potential of course management systems? Why do lectures remain the predominant form of in-class teaching when there is so much evidence to show that this is not an effective teaching style? As Barone explains, "Decision making within higher education suffers from conventions and timetables that assume institutions have not months, but years, to adapt to changes in their environments" (2005,

14.7). Consequently, change comes slowly to the academy, even though the young students it is committed to educating are one of the most adaptive, flexible segments of the American population. Such irony.

Although we librarians are limited in what we can do to bring about change to higher education, academic libraries can take the initiative to bring their culture, operations, services, and resources into better alignment with an environment of accelerating change. If this is done well, the library will become a model and a source of best practices for the rest of campus. There is no guaranteed formula for how to accomplish this, but we can consider some guiding principles.

Adopting an R&D Culture

If we take the view that the lengthy and successful past of academic libraries guarantees their future, then we should "stay the course" and continue to do business in much the same way, with perhaps some minor changes along the edges. If instead we believe that academic libraries need to reexamine and reconsider both what they do and how, then the culture of "stay the course" must be transformed into an "R&D" mind-set.

Research and development (R&D) means something quite different for an academic library than it does for a pharmaceutical firm. In an academic library setting, an R&D culture takes the form of continually evaluating, examining, and assessing your services, resources, and staffing to ensure that they meet the teaching, learning, and research needs of your academic institution.

An academic library that has embraced an R&D culture is one where the staff is constantly striving to stay current and bring new ideas into the organization. Although most libraries are doing this to some extent, this should be a core task for everyone in the organization. We may give lip service to the importance of staying current, reading the literature, and attending conferences and workshops, but do we provide the time, resources, and encouragement to accomplish these tasks? Are these a part of the normal work-week or something to be done when all of the "regular" duties are finished? The research component of R&D should be a regular duty of everyone on the staff, with mechanisms in place to capture the many great ideas that will emerge.

It is important to recognize that many new ideas will and should come from outside academic librarianship. In addition to following the library literature and attending library conferences, we need to stay abreast of trends and initiatives in higher education in general and in the information technology and management industry. On the one hand, we need to keep tabs on our potential competitors (e.g., Google and Amazon.com) and our potential partners (e.g., Google and Amazon.com). On the other hand, we should be attuned to the forces at play in higher education and how an academic library can interact with them.

It is not enough, however, to stimulate a research mind-set among your staff. Once the ideas start to flow, mechanisms must be in place to provide ways to experiment and explore their potential. This requires funding, flexibility of schedule and job duties, and, most important, a shared understanding that it is okay for an experiment to fail. Often when an idea for a new service, for example, is proposed, the question that comes in response is "What are you not going to do in order to fund or staff this?" This scenario does not encourage experimentation; rather, it reinforces the status quo.

To truly embrace R&D culture, academic libraries need "sandboxes" where staff can experiment and explore without consequence. If an idea emerges from the sandbox as successful, then the negotiations about trade-offs should happen, but at least at this point there is some evidence and facts on which to base the decisions. The sandbox will require funds to be set aside for the experiments and organizational flexibility to give the staff the time and support they need to conduct them. For some libraries, the experiments may naturally fall more toward the exploration of digital libraries, but not all experiments should concern new technologies. You could also be experimenting with new furniture (e.g., beanbags and gaming rockers), services (e.g., free coffee at the circulation desk), processes (e.g., self-checkout), or staffing (e.g., inviting writing tutors to sit with librarians at the reference desk).

The objective is to build an environment among your library staff that encourages thinking "outside the box" and nurtures ideas with potential. A library with an R&D mind-set will naturally be more agile and flexible and have a greater tolerance for change than one that adheres to a "stay the course" approach. The R&D atmosphere will be less orderly, with new ideas and experiments flowing from all levels of the staff, but the discomfort will be far milder than when the library suddenly finds that it must make a major course correction with little warning.

Rethinking "Library as Place"

The phrase "library as place" is one that has gained popularity over the past few years. But exactly what it means is something that should receive regular thought. "Library as place" may refer to the physical place where students come to engage in their academic endeavors. The library represents the place where students come to study, research, and engage in the discourse of the disciplines. This designation is in many ways quite limiting, however, because an academic library has the potential to be much more on campus.

Students are mobile, as is their technology. "Portable storage and wireless connections allow people to shift the way they spend their time with media and the places in which they consume media and information" (Rainie 2006), and this flexibility is welcomed, embraced, and expected by students. Activities are no longer tightly tied to places on campus, as they once were. Technologies such as cell phones and instant messaging are bringing about the convergence of the academic and social activities of a Net Generation student's life.

Students expect to read, eat, drink, sleep, socialize, engage in group and individual study, and use technology for both academic and social pursuits in nearly every place on campus. They direct these expectations to the campus library, in particular, because it is one of the main campus facilities with long operating hours and lots of seating. Consequently, the campus library does not have to be a "place" just for research, study, and other academic pursuits, though embracing this expanded role has implications for facilities, policies, and what technology is offered and how.

An easy example is a library's food and drink policy. Some libraries still prohibit students from bringing food and drinks into the library; others have brought Starbuck's cafés into the building. The former policy sends the message that the library is a place for short visits—where you can study and do research until you need a refreshment break. The latter invites students to stay longer—to settle in and make the library their "home away from dorm." In other words, the food and drink go a long way toward making the library the students' "third place," as described in chapter 3. Academic libraries may not always be about paper books and journals, but there is no reason that they cannot continue as the academic and social hub on campus.

Accepting That the Library Is Not the Virtual Place

Another way to consider the library as place is as a virtual place or destination for students. We must acknowledge, though, that a library's web presence is probably not going to become the destination of choice of our Net Generation students. An interesting recent OCLC finding is that college students seem relatively unfamiliar with the online presence of their academic libraries (De Rosa et al. 2005). Books are still strongly associated with academic libraries, and the billions of dollars spent to acquire online access to the scholarly literature appear to go quite unnoticed.

Miller (2006a) suggests that the more likely online, academic home of students is the university's portal or course management system. Consequently, libraries

> should be looking to expose library services there, both in terms of basic account information, but also by tying library holdings closely to course reading lists, etc. in order to make it as easy as possible for students to discover and gain access to library resources of use to them.

In the online world, we can no longer demand that students come to us exclusively for their academic resource needs, because there are now viable alternatives. Instead, we should be doing everything we can to bring the library to the students, both physically and virtually:

> We should integrate into the workflows that they [students] already undertake, and we should implement methods that make library content visible and relevant to those who might never have thought to turn to a library for anything more than a warm place to check their email. (Miller 2006a)

The objective can be expressed with the concept of academic library as traveling companion on the Web rather than as discrete virtual location.

As students discover references to books, articles, newspapers, or films while surfing the Web, they may want to know if their campus library owns those resources. At present, they usually accomplish this by writing down the citation, going to the library website, and searching across the many silos of resources the library owns. Technologies such as AJAX and Greasemonkey are providing far better alternatives.

For example, as a member of a university community, a student's credentials and rights, such as access to an article database, should be made evident wherever the student travels on the Web. An example of this is LibX (www.libx.org), an extension for the Firefox Internet browser developed by the Virginia Tech University Libraries. In addition to adding a toolbar to your browser that includes a search box for your library's catalog and access to your OpenURL resolver, LibX puts localized cues in web pages you visit—Amazon .com or Barnes and Noble, for example—if the library has resources related to that page. LibX alters and personalizes relevant websites, including Google and the *New York Times Book Review*, to reflect what your academic library has to offer.

As Murray (2006) explains:

> The library service must find users at their point of need, wherever that is: Users are on the Web; they are using their suite of office applications; students are using their e-learning environments; doctors are in their clinical management

systems; researchers are in their electronic lab books—this is where the library service has to meet them if it is to realise its full value.

Technology is no longer the barrier to actualizing this ideal. Instead, the barrier is the reluctance of academic libraries to disaggregate their content and services and allow users to take some control over where and how they want to engage their online library. We cannot control where students go on the Web to get information and gather resources for their studies, but we can certainly make it easier for them to bring their academic library along with them.

Supporting Authorship in the Digital Age

Net Generation students are developing a very different understanding of authorship than has been the norm up until now. Blogs, wikis, and Facebook, among other services, are challenging the once clear delineation between author and reader. Moreover, authorship is no longer a rare, privileged activity. "If you add up all the possible ways that teens might have created and shared content online, some 57% of all teen Internet users have contributed a creation of theirs to the online 'commons'" (Rainie 2006). More than half of our Net Generation students can rightfully claim to be authors, which has some interesting implications for libraries.

Through writing Amazon.com book reviews, adding comments to the blogs of their favorite novelists, and posting messages on the MySpace bulletin boards of their favorite musicians, Net Generation students have developed a sense that their opinion and input are both valued and welcomed into the conversation. As mentioned in chapters 4 and 5, libraries can make use of blogs, wikis, and tagging to engage students by inviting and encouraging them to enter into the discourse and share their thoughts. Rather than dissuade students of their self-identification as authors, we should be encouraging it.

Unfortunately, this blurring of authorship has also blurred the understanding of copyright. Students have what Hilton describes as a "rip, mix, and burn" mentality: "Today's students want to be able to take content from other people. They want to mix it, in new creative ways—to produce it, to publish it, and to distribute it. Technology allows them to do that" (2006, 60). The Recording Industry Association of America and the Motion Picture Association of America would like academic libraries and the rest of campus to help police violations of copyright, but there is a much more productive, appropriate role for libraries to play here. Although we cannot do much to change the "rip, mix, and burn" practices of our students, we can strive to supply the tools and copyright-friendly content with which to do this appropriately. In addition to text, students need an ample supply of images, videos, and audio files with which to experiment and create. This requires a different kind of collection development mind-set and new language in our licensing contracts, but who on campus is better positioned to fulfill this need?

Understanding Our Users

Academic librarians cannot rest on the knowledge that Net Generation students do things differently. To continue to support the teaching, learning, and research needs of students through active participation in the creation, transmission, and dissemination of knowledge, we need to know both how they are different and why. Rettig described our charge this way:

> Just as we are experts in information storage, access, retrieval, and systems, we need to become expert anthropologists of our user communities. Through study we need to learn their information-handling habits—their knowledge of the information universe, their understanding and misunderstanding of its inner workings, their appreciation and ignorance of the implications of those inner workings for their academic work. By knowing their values, assumptions, and knowledge of information issues, we can develop resources that respond to those values, assumptions, and knowledge but that do not affirm their whole assumptions. (2003, 20)

To the degree it is successful, this book demonstrates how a rich understanding of how and why students use a technology, such as online games, can illuminate new ways academic libraries can realign and improve their services, staffing, facilities, and resources. And although much of this information can be pulled from national surveys and reports, such as those by the Pew Internet and American Life Project, OCLC, and EDUCAUSE, these are no substitutes for knowledge of your local environment.

At the University of Rochester Libraries we have been quite fortunate to have anthropologist Nancy Fried Foster on staff. She has taught, and continues to teach, us different methodologies by which we can gain new insights into our university community. Following a one-year study of faculty funded by the Institute of Museum and Library Services, the libraries funded from the existing operating budget a two-year study of undergraduate students. In trying to answer the question "How do students research and write papers?" we engaged them in reflective interviews and intellectual self-assessments. We asked them to create maps of their movements on campus and take pictures. We invited them to codesign library spaces and express their wants and needs for academic and social spaces. And all the while we quietly observed them, using the field observation techniques Foster taught us.[1]

The results of this undergraduate research project are quite numerous. The transcriptions of hundreds of hours of interviews can be mined again and again for new insights. The photographs the students took, such as "a favorite place to study" or "someplace in the library where you feel lost," provide a baseline from which we can assess improvements to the physical library. We also have a far better understanding of the research and writing process and how difficult it can be to separate the two.

Most important, the more than thirty library staff who participated in the project in one way or another have a far better understanding and appreciation of our Net Generation students. And from this understanding springs new, innovative ideas. Moreover, we have come to understand how easy it can be to gather student input, and we are no longer hesitant or shy to do so. A new philosophy of "don't guess, just ask" has helped us place our students in the center of our design process, whether the objective is a service, website design, or facility renovation. Consequently, we can say with confidence that our academic library is aligned with the needs of our Net Generation students.

Not every academic library needs an anthropologist on staff. But each needs to find some way to increase its understanding of its student body. For example, the MIT Libraries (Bartley et al. 2006) and several academic libraries in Denmark (Akselbo et al. 2006) have used cultural probes, field studies, case studies, surveys, and interviews to study their local student populations. The New York University Libraries completed a study of the needs of their faculty and graduate students (Marcus, Covert-Vail, and Mandel 2007), as did the University of Minnesota Libraries (2006). Kennedy (2006) recommends creating personas to represent the different segments of your library patron base. The list of methodologies and techniques continues to grow.

Maness (2006) puts it bluntly: "As communities change, libraries must not only change with them, they must allow users to change the library." Projecting our college experiences onto today's students no longer works. Whether we call it a generation gap or a digital divide, the results are fundamental differences in the way information is sought and gathered, social networks are formed and sustained, and knowledge is created and disseminated. These all go to the heart of the mission of an academic library and, consequently, cannot be ignored or dismissed.

By the time this book is published, much of the information about the specific technologies addressed, such as online gaming, wikis, and tagging, will be dated—another unfortunate consequence of the accelerating pace of technology advancements. Still, the five guiding principles reviewed above should hold true for some time to come. If embraced, they will position an academic library to be ready and open for the next disruptive technology while remaining focused on its core mission. The result will be a vibrant and exciting future for academic libraries.

NOTE

1. An edited volume that describes the various methodologies and significant findings will be published by ACRL in September 2007; it is tentatively titled *Studying Students: The Undergraduate Research Project at the University of Rochester.*

REFERENCES

Agrawal, Ravi. 2006. Social networking fuels new web boom. *CNN.Com: The Briefing Room,* October 3. http://www.cnn.com/2006/TECH/internet/10/03/social.networking/index.html.

Akselbo, Jeppe Lomholt, et al. 2006. *The hybrid library: From the users' perspective.* A report from the DEFF project. http://www.statsbiblioteket.dk/site/readpdf.jsp?PDF=/publ/fieldstudies.pdf.

Allen, Laurie, and Michael Winkler. 2006. PennTags: Social bookmarking in a university library. EDUCAUSE 2006 conference presentation. http://www.slideshare.net/laurie.allen/penntags-presentation-at-educause-2006.

Anderson, Chris. 2006. *The long tail: Why the future of business is selling less of more.* New York: Hyperion.

Arrington, Michael. 2005. TechCrunch: 85% of college students use Facebook. September 7. http://www.techcrunch.com/2005/09/07/85-of-college-students-use-facebook/.

Associated Press. 2003. Fire up that game, boy. *Wired News,* May 28. http://www.wired.com/news/culture/games/0,59016-0.html.

Barone, Carole. 2005. The new academy. In *Educating the net generation,* ed. Diana G. Oblinger and James L. Oblinger. Boulder, CO: EDUCAUSE. http://www.educause.edu/ir/library/pdf/pub7101n.pdf.

Bartley, Maggie, et al. 2006. *User needs assessment of information seeking activities of MIT students—Spring 2006.* Boston: MIT Libraries. http://hdl.handle.net/1721.1/33456.

Blyberg, John. 2006. More than just faith: Radical trust. May 21. http://www.blyberg.net/2006/05/21/more-than-just-faith-radical-trust/.

Branston, Christy. 2006. From game studies to bibliographic gaming: Libraries tap into the video game culture. *Bulletin of the American Society for Information Science and Technology* 32 (4): 24–26, 29.

Brightman, James. 2006. Study: Women gamers outnumber men in the 25–30 age group. *GameDaily Biz,* April 17. http://biz.gamedaily.com/industry/feature/?id=12424.

Brown, John Seely. 2002. The social life of learning: How can continuing education be reconfigured in the future? *Continuing Higher Education Review* 66:50–69.

Brown, John Seely, and Paul Duguid. 2000. *The social life of information.* Boston: Harvard Business School Press.

Bruce, Harry, William Jones, and Susan Dumais. 2004. Information behavior that keeps found things found. *Information Research* 10 (1). http://informationr.net/ir/10-1/paper207.html.

Business Week. 1975. The office of the future. June 30, 48–70.

Carnevale, Dan. 2006. E-mail is for old people. *Chronicle of Higher Education* 53 (7): A27. http://chronicle.com/weekly/v53/i07/07a02701.htm.

Caruso, Judith B., and Robert B. Kvavik. 2005. *ECAR study of students and information technology, 2005: Convenience, connection, control, and learning.* ECAR Research Study no. 6. Boulder, CO: EDUCAUSE. http://www.educause.edu/ir/library/pdf/ers0506/rs/ERS0506w.pdf.

Casey, Michael E., and Laura C. Savastinuk. 2006. Library 2.0. *Library Journal* 131 (14). http://www.libraryjournal.com/article/CA6365200.html.

Castronova, Edward. 2001. *Virtual worlds: A first-hand account of market and society on the cyberian frontier.* Munich, Germany: Center for Economic Studies and Information Institute for Economic Research, 618. http://papers.ssrn.com/abstract=294828.

————. 2005. *Synthetic worlds: The business and culture of online games.* Chicago: University of Chicago Press.

Chad, Ken, and Paul Miller. 2005. *Do libraries matter? The rise of Library 2.0.* Birmingham, UK: Talis Information Limited. http://www.talis.com/downloads/white_papers/DoLibrariesMatter.pdf.

Christensen, Clayton M. 2000. *The innovator's dilemma.* New York: Harper Business.

Christensen, Clayton M., Sally Aaron, and William Clark. 2001. Disruption in education. In *The Internet and the university: 2001.* Boulder, CO: EDUCAUSE. http://www.educause.edu/apps/forum/ffpiu01w.asp.

College Parents of America. 2006. Survey of current college parent experiences, March 30, 2006. Press release. http://www.collegeparents .org/cpa/about-press.html?n=1310.

Collins, Jim. 2001. *Good to great.* New York: HarperCollins.

———. 2005. *Good to great and the social sectors: A monograph to accompany good to great.* Boulder, CO: Jim Collins.

Corrado, Edward M., Heather L. Moulaison, and Eric Thul. 2006. Integrating RSS feeds of new library acquisitions into a course management system. Paper presented at VALE Users' Conference, Rutgers University. http:// www.tcnj.edu/~corrado/scholarly/vale2006/vale2006_combined.pdf.

Crawford, Walt. 2006. Folksonomy and dichotomy. *Cites and Insights* 6 (4): 1–3. http://citesandinsights.info/civ6i4.pdf.

De Rosa, Cathy, Joanne Cantrell, Diane Cellentani, and Janet Hawk. 2005. *Perceptions of libraries and information resources: A report to the OCLC membership.* Dublin, OH: OCLC Online Computer Library Center, Inc. http://www.oclc.org/reports/2005perceptions.htm.

Dede, Chris. 2005. Planning for neomillennial learning styles: Implications for investments in technology and faculty. In *Educating the net generation,* ed. Diana G. Oblinger and James L. Oblinger. Boulder, CO: EDUCAUSE. http://www.educause.edu/ir/library/pdf/pub7101o.pdf.

Dempsey, Lorcan. 2006. Four pictures and a conclusion: The third age of libraries in a network environment. Paper presented at Taiga Forum, March, Chicago. http://www.oclc.org/research/presentations/ dempsey/taiga.ppt.

Dillon, Sam. 2005. At public universities, warnings of privatization. *New York Times,* October 16, 12.

Drew, Wilfred. 2005. Chat reference at Morrisville State College Library. http://babyboomerlibrarian.blogspot.com/2005/05/chat-reference-at-morrisville-state.html.

EDUCAUSE Learning Initiative. 2005. Seven things you should know about . . . social bookmarking. Boulder, CO: EDUCAUSE. http://www .educause.edu/ir/library/pdf/ELI7001.pdf.

———. 2006. Seven things you should know about . . . virtual worlds. Boulder, CO: EDUCAUSE. http://www.educause.edu/ir/library/pdf/ ELI7015.pdf.

Etches-Johnson, Amanda. 2006. The brave new world of social bookmarking: Everything you always wanted to know but were too afraid to ask. *Feliciter* 52 (2): 56–58.

Ferris, S. Pixy, and Hilary Wilder. 2006. Uses and potentials of wikis in the classroom. *Innovate: Journal of Online Education* 2 (5). http://www .innovateonline.info/index.php?view=article&id=258.

Foster, Andrea L. 2006. Harvard to offer law course in "virtual world." *Chronicle of Higher Education* 53 (3): A20.

Foster, Nancy, and Susan Gibbons. 2005. Understanding faculty to improve content recruitment for institutional repositories. *D-Lib Magazine* 11 (1). http://www.dlib.org/dlib/january05/foster/01foster.html.

Gallaway, Beth. 2005. What libraries can do for gamers (other than programming and collections). Paper presented at Gaming, Learning and Libraries Symposium, Chicago. http://gaminginlibraries.org/ 2005symposium/presentations/bethgallaway.pdf.

Gee, James Paul. 2003. *What video games have to teach us about learning and literacy.* New York: Palgrave Macmillan.

———. 2005. High score education: Games, not school, are teaching kids to think. *Wired* 11 (5). http://www.wired.com/wired/archive/11.05/view .html?pg=1.

Giles, Jim. 2005. Internet encyclopedias go head to head. *Nature* 438 (December 15). http://www.nature.com/nature/journal/v438/n7070/full/ 438900a.html.

Golder, Scott A., and Bernardo A. Huberman. 2006. Usage patterns of collaborative tagging systems. *Journal of Information Science* 32 (2): 198–208.

Goodwin, C. 1994. Professional vision. *American Anthropologist,* n.s., 96 (3): 606–33.

Gordon-Murnane, Laura. 2006. Social bookmarking, folksonomies, and Web 2.0 tools. *Searcher* 14 (6): 26–38.

Graetz, Ken A. 2006. The psychology of learning environments. *EDUCAUSE Review* 41 (6): 60–75. http://www.educause.edu/ir/library/pdf/ erm0663.pdf.

Green, C. Shawn, and Daphne Bavelier. 2003. Action video game modifies visual selective attention. *Nature* 423 (May 29): 534–37.

Griffiths, Mark D., Mark N. O. Davies, and Darren Chappell. 2003. Breaking the stereotype: The case of online gaming. *CyberPsychology and Behavior* 6 (1): 81–91.

Guenther, Kim. 2005. Socializing your website with wikis, twikis, and blogs. *Online* 29 (6): 51–53.

Guy, Marieke, and Emma Tonkin. 2006. Folksonomies: Tidying up tags? *D-Lib Magazine* 12 (1). http://www.dlib.org/dlib/january06/guy/01guy .htm.

Hammond, Tony, Timo Hannay, Ben Lund, and Joanna Scott. 2005. Social bookmarking tools (I). *D-Lib Magazine* 11 (4). http://www.dlib.org/dlib/april05/hammond/04hammond.html.

Harder, Geoff. 2006. Connecting the dots: Social software and the social nature of libraries. *Feliciter* 2:54–55.

Hartman, Joel, Patsy Moskal, and Chuck Dziuban. 2005. Preparing the academy of today for the learner of tomorrow. In *Educating the net generation*, ed. Diana G. Oblinger and James L. Oblinger. Boulder, CO: EDUCAUSE. http://www.educause.edu/ir/library/pdf/pub7101f.pdf.

Hawkins, Donald T., and Barbara Brynko. 2006. Gaming: The next hot technology for libraries? *Information Today* 23 (6): 1, 51.

Hemp, Paul. 2006. Avatar-based marketing. *Harvard Business Review* 84 (6): 48–57.

Hilton, James. 2006. The future for higher education: Sunrise or perfect storm? *EDUCAUSE Review* 41 (2): 58–71.

Howe, Neil, and William Strauss. 2000. *Millennials rising: The next great generation.* New York: Vintage Books.

Israel, Betsy. 2006. The overconnecteds. *New York Times,* November 5, 4a: 20–23.

Johnson, Steven. 2005. *Everything bad is good for you: How today's popular culture is actually making us smarter.* New York: Penguin.

Jones, Steve. 2002. *The Internet goes to college: How students are living in the future with today's technology.* Washington, DC: Pew Internet and American Life Project. http://www.usdla.org/html/journal/OCT02_Issue/index.html.

Kennedy, Mary Lee. 2006. The library as the user sees it. *SirsiDynix,* July 27. http://www.imakenews.com/sirsi/e_article000627222.cfm?x=b5dRbWJ,b2rpQhRM,w.

Kenney, Anne, Nancy McGovern, Ida Martinez, and Lance Heidig. 2003. Google meets eBay: What academic librarians can learn from alternative information providers. *D-Lib Magazine* 9 (6). http://www.dlib.org/dlib/june03/kenney/06kenney.html.

Kolbert, Elizabeth. 2001. Pimps and dragons: How an online world survived a social breakdown. *New Yorker,* May 28, 88.

Kroski, Ellyssa. 2005. The hive mind: Folksonomies and user-based tagging. December 7. Blog ed. http://infotangle.blogsome.com/2005/12/07/the-hive-mind-folksonomies-and-user-based-tagging/.

Kurweil, Ray. 1999. *The age of spiritual machines.* New York: Penguin.

Kvavik, Robert B. 2005. Convenience, communications, and control: How students use technology. In *Educating the net generation,* ed. Diana G. Oblinger and James L. Oblinger. Boulder, CO: EDUCAUSE. http://www.educause.edu/ir/library/pdf/pub7101g.pdf.

Kvavik, Robert B., Judith B. Caruso, and Glenda Morgan. 2004. *ECAR study of students and information technology, 2004: Convenience, connection, and control.* ECAR Research Study no. 5. Boulder, CO: EDUCAUSE. http://www.educause.edu/ir/library/pdf/ers0405/rs/ers0405w.pdf.

Laber, Emily. 2001. Men are from Quake, women are from Ultima. *New York Times,* January 11, G1.

Lafferty, Susan, and Jenny Edwards. 2004. Disruptive technologies: What future universities and their libraries? *Library Management* 25 (6–7): 252–58.

Lanchester, John. 2006. A bigger bang. *Guardian,* November 4. http://www.guardian.co.uk/weekend/story/0,,1937496,00.html.

Lankes, R. David, and Joanne Silverstein. 2006. *Participatory networks: The library as conversation.* Syracuse, NY: Information Institute of Syracuse. http://iis.syr.edu/projects/PNOpen/.

Lenhart, A., and S. Fox. 2006. *Bloggers: A portrait of the Internet's new storytellers.* Washington, DC: Pew Internet and American Life Project. http://www.pewinternet.org/pdfs/PIP%20Bloggers%20Report%20July%2019%202006.pdf.

Lenhart, Amanda, Mary Madden, and Paul Hitlin. 2005. *Teens and technology: Youth are leading the transition to a fully wired and mobile nation.* Washington, DC: Pew Internet and American Life Project. http://www.pewinternet.org/pdfs/PIP_Teens_Tech_July2005web.pdf.

Lewis, David W. 2004. *The Innovator's Dilemma:* Disruptive change and academic libraries. *Library Administration and Management* 18 (2): 68–74. http://hdl.handle.net/1805/173.

Lippincott, Joan. 2005. Net generation students and libraries. In *Educating the net generation,* ed. Diana G. Oblinger and James L. Oblinger. Boulder, CO: EDUCAUSE. http://www.educause.edu/ir/library/pdf/pub7101m.pdf.

Lund, Ben, Tony Hammond, Martin Flack, and Timo Hannay. 2005. Social bookmarking tools (II). *D-Lib Magazine* 11 (4). http://www.dlib.org/dlib/april05/lund/04lund.html.

Lupien, Pascal. 2006. Virtual reference in the age of pop-up blockers, firewalls, and Service Pack 2. *Online* 30 (4). http://www.infotoday.com/online/jul06/Lupien.shtml.

Maness, Jack M. 2006. Library 2.0 theory: Web 2.0 and its implications for libraries. *Webology* 3 (2). http://www.webology.ir/2006/v3n2/a25.html.

Marcus, Cecily, Lucinda Covert-Vail, and Carol A. Mandel. 2007. NYU 21st Century Library Project: Designing a research library of the future for New York University. http://library.nyu.edu/about/KPLReport.pdf.

Mathews, Brian. 2006a. Do you Facebook? Networking with students online. *College and Research Libraries News* 67 (5): 306.

———. 2006b. Intuitive revelations: The ubiquitous reference model. http://hdl.handle.net/1853/8446.

———. 2006c. Sin, death and resurrection: A Facebook update. December. http://theubiquitouslibrarian.typepad.com/the_ubiquitous_librarian/2006/12/sin_death_resur.html.

———. 2006d. What to do when Facebook closes down your library storefront. October. http://theubiquitouslibrarian.typepad.com/the_ubiquitous_librarian/2006/10/what_to_do_when.html.

Matier, Michael W., and C. Clinton Sidle. 1992. *Developing a strategic plan for library space needs through 2010.* ED349024. http://eric.ed.gov/ERICWebPortal/contentdelivery/servlet/ERICServlet?accno=ED349024.

McCulley, Lucretia, and Olivia Reinauer. 2006. Connecting with AIM: The search for a virtual reference niche. Paper presented at LOEX 2006, University of Maryland. http://library.richmond.edu/information/LOEX06%20Paper.pdf.

McGrath, Dennis, and Doug Hill. 2004. UnrealTriage: A game-based simulation for emergency response. Paper presented at Huntsville Simulation Conference. http://www.ists.dartmouth.edu/library/58.pdf.

Miller, Paul. 2005. Web 2.0: Building the new library. *Ariadne* 45 (October 30). http://www.ariadne.ac.uk/issue45/miller/.

———. 2006a. Coming together around Library 2.0: A focus for discussion and a call to arms. *D-Lib Magazine* 12 (4). http://www.dlib.org/dlib/april06/miller/04miller.html.

———. 2006b. *Library 2.0: The challenge of disruptive innovation.* Birmingham, UK: Talis Information. http://www.talis.com/resources/documents/447_Library_2_prf1.pdf.

Murray, Robin. 2006. Library systems: Synthesise, specialise, mobilise. *Ariadne* 48 (July). http://www.ariadne.ac.uk/issue48/murray/.

National Center for Education Statistics. 2005. *The condition of education 2005.* Washington, DC. http://purl.access.gpo.gov.ezp.lib.rochester.edu/GPO/LPS33497.

Nicholson, Peter J. 2006. The changing role of intellectual authority. Paper presented at the Association of Research Libraries' 148th Membership Meeting, Ottawa, Canada, May 18.

Oblinger, Diana, and James Oblinger. 2005. Is it age or IT: First steps towards understanding the net generation. In *Educating the net generation,* ed. Diana G. Oblinger and James L. Oblinger. Boulder, CO: EDUCAUSE. http://www.educause.edu/ir/library/pdf/pub7101b.pdf.

Oldenburg, Ray. 1999. *The great good place: Cafes, coffee shops, bookstores, bars, hair salons, and other hangouts at the heart of a community.* New York: Marlowe.

Onwuegbuzie, Anthony J., Qun G. Jiao, and Sharon L. Bostick. 2004. *Library anxiety: Theory, research, and applications.* Lanham, MD: Scarecrow Press.

O'Reilly, Tim. 2005. What is Web 2.0: Design patterns and business models for the next generation software. http://www.oreillynet.com/pub/a/oreilly/tim/news/2005/09/30/what-is-web-20.html.

Poe, Marshall. 2006. The hive. *Atlantic Online,* September. http://www.theatlantic.com/doc/200609/wikipedia/.

Prensky, Marc. 2001. Digital natives, digital immigrants. *On the Horizon* 9 (5): 1–6.

———. 2005. What can you learn from a cell phone? Almost anything! *Innovate* 1 (5). http://www.innovateonline.info/index.php?view=article&id=83.

Rainie, Lee. 2005. *The state of blogging.* Washington, DC: Pew Internet and American Life Project. http://www.pewinternet.org/pdfs/PIP_blogging_data.pdf.

———. 2006. *Life online: Teens and technology and the world to come.* Speech ed. http://www.pewinternet.org/ppt/Teens%20and%20technology.pdf.

Rettig, James. 2003. Technology, cluelessness, anthropology, and the memex: The future of academic reference service. *Reference Services Review* 31 (1): 17–21.

Roberts, Gregory R. 2005. Technology and learning expectations of the net generation. In *Educating the net generation,* ed. Diana G. Oblinger and James L. Oblinger. Boulder, CO: EDUCAUSE. http://www.educause.edu/ir/library/pdf/pub7101c.pdf.

Selingo, Jeffrey. 2005. Leaders' views about higher education, their jobs, and their lives. *Chronicle of Higher Education,* November 4, Special Report. http://chronicle.com/weekly/v52/i11/11a02601.htm.

Sellers, Patricia. 2006. MySpace cowboys. *Fortune,* September 4. http://
money.cnn.com/magazines/fortune/fortune_archive/2006/09/04/
8384727/index.htm.

Shiu, Eulynn, and Amanda Lenhart. 2004. *How Americans use instant messaging.* Washington, DC: Pew Internet and American Life Project. http://
www.pewinternet.org/pdfs/PIP_Instantmessage_Report.pdf.

Simmons, Michelle Holschuh. 2005. Librarians as disciplinary discourse
mediators: Using genre theory to move toward critical information
literacy. *Portal: Libraries and the Academy* 5 (3): 297–311.

Sinha, Rashmi. 2005. A cognitive analysis of tagging (or how the lower
cognitive cost of tagging makes it popular). September 27. http://www
.rashmisinha.com/archives/05_09/tagging-cognitive.html.

Squire, Kurt. In press. Civilization III as a world history sandbox. In
Civilization and its discontents: Virtual history, real fantasies. Milan, Italy:
Ludologica Press. http://education.mit.edu/11127/civ3-education-
chapter.doc.

Squire, Kurt, and Henry Jenkins. 2003. Harnessing the power of games in
education. *Insight* 3 (5). http://website.education.wisc.edu/kdsquire/
manuscripts/insight.pdf.

Squire, Kurt, and Constance Steinkuehler. 2005. Meet the gamers. *Library
Journal* 130 (7): 38–41.

Standage, Tom. 2006. The culture war: How new media keeps corrupting
our children. *Wired* 14 (4): 114–15. http://www.wired.com/wired/
archive/14.04/war_pr.html.

Steinkuehler, Constance A. 2004. Learning in massive multiplayer online
games. In *Proceedings of the Sixth International Conference of the Learning
Sciences,* ed. Y. B. Kafai et al. Mahwah, NJ: Erlbaum. http://website
.education.wisc.edu/steinkuehler/papers/SteinkuehlerICLS2004.pdf.

———. 2005. The new third place: Massively multiplayer online gaming
in American youth culture. *Tidskrift för Lärarutbildning och Forskning* 12
(3): 16–33. http://website.education.wisc.edu/steinkuehler/papers/
SteinkuehlerTIDSKRIFT2005.pdf.

Steinkuehler, Constance, and Dmitri Williams. 2006. Where everybody
knows your (screen) name: Online games as "third places." *Journal of
Computer-Mediated Communication* 11 (4). http://jcmc.indiana.edu/vol11/
issue4/steinkuehler.html.

Stephens, Michael. 2006. Web 2.0 and libraries: Best practices for social
software. *Library Technology Reports* 42 (4).

Strauss, William, and Neil Howe. 2006. *Millennials and the pop culture.* Great Falls, VA: Life Course Associates.

Sutton, Lynn, and H. David "Giz" Womack. 2006. Got game? Hosting a game night in an academic library. *College and Research Libraries News* 67 (3): 173–76.

Svaboda, Elizabeth. 2006. A brief history of game time. *Wired* 14 (4): 132.

Tapscott, Don. 1997. *Growing up digital: The rise of the net generation.* New York: McGraw-Hill.

Taylor, T. L. 2003. Multiple pleasures: Women and online gaming. *Convergence* 9 (1): 21–46.

———. 2006. *Play between worlds: Exploring online game culture.* Cambridge, MA: MIT Press.

Terdiman, Daniel. 2004. Campus life comes to Second Life. *Wired News,* September 24. http://www.wired.com/news/games/1,65052-0.html.

Thomas, Chuck, and Robert H. McDonald. 2005. Millennial net value(s): Disconnects between libraries and the information age mindset. Tallahassee: Florida State University D-Scholarship Repository. http://dscholarship.lib.fsu.edu/general/4.

Tonkin, Emma. 2005. Making the case for a wiki. *Ariadne* 42 (January 30). http://www.ariadne.ac.uk/issue42/tonkin/intro.html.

———. 2006. Folksonomies: The fall and rise of plain-text tagging. *Ariadne* 47 (April). http://www.ariadne.ac.uk/issue47/tonkin/.

Twenge, Jean M. 2006. *Generation me: Why today's young Americans are more confident, assertive, entitled—and more miserable—than ever before.* New York: Free Press.

University of Minnesota Libraries. 2006. A multi-dimensional framework for academic support: A final report. http://www.lib.umn.edu/about/mellon/UMN_Multi-dimensional_Framework_Final_Report.pdf.

Van Eck, Richard. 2006. Digital game-based learning: It's not just the digital natives who are restless. *EDUCAUSE Review* 41 (2): 16–30. http://www.educause.edu/ir/library/pdf/erm0620.pdf.

Van Orsdel, Lee C., and Kathleen Born. 2005. Choosing sides: Periodical price survey 2005. *Library Journal* 130 (7): 43–48.

Vanden Boogart, Matthew Robert. 2006. Uncovering the social impacts of Facebook on a college campus. Master's thesis. Kansas State University. http://hdl.handle.net/2097/181.

Wager, James. 2005. Support services for the net generation. In *Educating the net generation,* ed. Diana G. Oblinger and James L. Oblinger. Boulder, CO: EDUCAUSE. http://www.educause.edu/ir/library/pdf/pub7101j.pdf.

Ward, David, and M. Kathleen Kern. 2006. Combining IM and vendor-based chat: A report from the frontlines of an integrated service. *Portal: Libraries and the Academy* 6 (4): 417–29.

Wenger, E. 1998. *Communities of practice: Learning, meaning, and identity.* New York: Cambridge University Press.

Whelan, David. 2006. The big picture. *Forbes* 178 (4): 44.

Williams, Alex. 2005. Do you MySpace? *New York Times,* August 28. http://www.nytimes.com/2005/08/28/fashion/sundaystyles/28MYSPACE.html.

Woodcock, Bruce. 2006. An analysis of MMOG subscription growth. http://www.mmogchart.com.

Woolley, Scott. 2006. Video fixation. *Forbes* 178 (8): 100–106.

Wright, Will. 2006. Dream machines: Will Wright explains how games are unleashing the human imagination. *Wired* 14 (4): 110–12. http://www.wired.com/wired/archive/14.04/wright.html.

Yee, Nick. 2001a. The Norrathian scrolls: A study of EverQuest. http://www.nickyee.com/eqt/home.html.

———. 2001b. Unmasking the avatar: The demographics of MMO player motivations, in-game preferences, and attrition. *Gamasutra,* September 21. http://www.gamasutra.com/resource_guide/20040920/yee_01.shtml.

———. 2004. The Daedalus Project: The psychology of MMORPGs. http://www.nickyee.com/daedalus/archives/000758.php.

INDEX

Susan Gibbons is associate dean for public services and collection development at the University of Rochester, River Campus Libraries. Ms. Gibbons earned an MLS and MA in history from Indiana University and a professional MBA from the University of Massachusetts. She is currently working on her EdD in higher education administration. She held library positions at Indiana University and the University of Massachusetts–Amherst before moving to Rochester, New York, in 1999. She has published on various topics including institutional repositories, electronic books, and course management systems. In 2005 she was named a *Library Journal* "Mover and Shaker" and in 2006 was a visiting program officer for the Association of Research Libraries. She is a 2003 fellow of the Frye Leadership Institute.

CREATING CREDIBILITY

LEGITIMACY AND ACCOUNTABILITY FOR TRANSNATIONAL CIVIL SOCIETY